ARMORED VICTORY
1945

ARMORED VICTORY 1945

U.S. ARMY TANK COMBAT IN THE EUROPEAN THEATER FROM THE BATTLE OF THE BULGE TO GERMANY'S SURRENDER

Steven Zaloga

STACKPOLE
BOOKS

Published by
STACKPOLE BOOKS
5067 Ritter Road
Mechanicsburg, PA 17055
www.stackpolebooks.com

10 9 8 7 6 5 4 3 2 1

Library of Congress Cataloging-in-Publication Data

Zaloga, Steve.
  Armored victory 1945 : U.S. Army tank combat in the European theater from the Battle of the Bulge to Germany's surrender / Steven Zaloga.
      p. cm.
  Includes index.
  ISBN 978-0-8117-0771-8
  1. World War, 1939–1945—Tank warfare. 2. World War, 1939–1945—Tank warfare—Pictorial works. 3. World War, 1939–1945—Campaigns—Western Front. 4. World War, 1939–1945—Campaigns—Western Front—Pictorial works. 5. United States. Army—Armored troops—History—World War, 1939–1945. 6. United States. Army—Armored troops—History—World War, 1939–1945—Pictorial works. I. Title.
  D793.Z343 2012
  940.54'21—dc23
                          2011039336

Contents

Introduction

THIS BOOK IS THE SECOND of a two-volume set covering U.S. Army armored units in combat in the European theater of operations from D-Day on 6 June 1944 through the end of the conflict in May 1945. The two volumes are split chronologically between 1944 and 1945. The aim of this book is to provide an in-depth visual record of armored combat through the eyes of the U.S. Army combat cameramen. Although the majority of the photos cover American armored vehicles, an extensive selection of photos of German vehicles is also included to help provide a more complete image of the fighting. However, the armored operations of the Field Marshal Bernard Montgomery's neighboring British-Canadian 21st Army Group are outside the scope of this book. Nor does this book cover U.S. armored units the Mediterranean theater of operations in Italy.

These photos come primarily from the main collection of World War II U.S. Army Signal Corps photos, which totals about a quarter of a million prints. This collection was initially housed at the Pentagon through the early 1970s when I first began to do my photo research. It was later transferred to the Defense Audio-Visual Agency facility at Bolling Air Force Base in Virginia and finally to the National Archives and Records Administration (NARA II) at College Park, Maryland, where it currently resides. The vast majority of the photos in this book come from this collection. A subsidiary Signal Corps collection resides at the U.S. Army Military History Institute at Carlisle Barracks, Pennsylvania, which also recently absorbed the rump Signal Corps collection held by the U.S. Army Cen-

ter for Military History. In most cases, these photos duplicate the National Archives' holdings. Although the Signal Corps collections contain most of the surviving World War II photos, they do not contain all of them.

Many photos shot by Signal Corps combat cameramen were released through other venues during the war, such as the Office of War Information. A large portion of these photos are available at NARA II. In addition, other photos were never accepted into the main Signal Corps collection but were retained by separate organizations. For example, the library at the U.S. Military Academy at West Point has the Bradley Collection, which is a separate and distinct collection of Signal Corps photos, some of which are not located in the main Signal Corps holdings at the National Archives or Military History Institute. Finally, there are a variety of other smaller holdings at various archives, including the Patton Museum Library, formerly at Fort Knox, Kentucky, and the Ordnance Museum, formerly at Aberdeen Proving Ground. Besides the U.S. Army collections, there are also some useful photos of U.S. Army operations in the U.S. Navy and U.S. Air Force collections. It has taken me nearly forty years of research to collect the photos in this book.

The Signal Corps photos sometimes, but not always, include basic information on the date, location, and units depicted in the photo. This data is incomplete—and sometimes quite erroneous. Unit information is often lacking, and the spelling of the European locations is notoriously erratic. For example, a series of photos identified as having been taken in Ploy, France, were actually taken in Parroy, France. Over the years, European military historians have done considerable work in more precisely identifying the actual location of these photos, and I have made every effort to try to correct this information when possible. However, a certain measure of uncertainty still remains about some of the details of many photos.

I have attempted to select the photos in this books to satisfy a variety of potential readers. I have included photos of interest to military historians covering significant battles. At the same time, I have attempted to include photos providing technical details that will appeal to military hobbyists such as military modelers, war-gamers, and historical reen-actors. It is very difficult to achieve an ideal balance because of the very uneven coverage in wartime photos. After decades of research in the Signal Corps photos, I quickly discovered that combat photos taken during or shortly after major battles—such as Omaha Beach on D-Day or the first few days of fighting in the Ardennes in December 1945—are actually quite rare. Other events attracted a disproportionate amount of attention, so photo coverage of the liberation of Paris on 25 August 1944 was quite thorough. I have included some photos of poor technical quality as I believe these will be of interest to readers. Likewise, in the captions, I have tried to reach a balance between historical and technical information.

CHAPTER 1

Crushing the Bulge

THE GERMAN OFFENSIVE in the Ardennes was stopped in the days after Christmas 1944. However, the fighting was far from over. During the first week of January 1945, Hitler attempted to secure some gains from the limited success in the Bastogne area and shifted the panzer forces of the Sixth Panzer Army from the failed northern sector to the Bastogne area. By this time, Lt. Gen. Courtney Hodges's U.S. First Army and Lt. Gen. George Patton's U.S. Third Army had moved up substantial reserves of armor, and the last-gasp German attacks were crushed. Hitler finally recognized the obvious, pulled back the Sixth Panzer Army, and sent it off to Hungary, where it became embroiled in an equally doomed offensive against the Red Army.

While the Germans realized that the Ardennes offensive had failed, they did not give up. January saw a brutal series of battles as the U.S. Army attempted to regain the territory lost in December. The enemy was as much the weather as the Germans, with particularly cold winter weather and deep snow hampering operations. On 16 January 1945, Patton's Third Army linked up with Hodges's First Army near Houffalize, and by 28 January, the last territory lost in the Battle of the Bulge was regained.

Losses in the Ardennes were heavy on both sides. American casualties totaled 75,482, of which 8,407 were killed, 46,170 wounded, and 20,905 missing through the end of January. The British 30 Corps lost 1,408, including 200 killed, 239 wounded, and 969 missing. Estimates of German losses vary from 67,200 to 98,025 casualties, depending on the parameters. The lower figure included 11,171 killed, 34,439 wounded, and 23,150 missing. The Wehrmacht lost about 610 tanks and assault guns in the Ardennes (about 45 percent of its original strength) compared to about 730 American tanks and tank destroyers (less than 20 percent of the force). The head of the German High Command West (OB West) staff later wrote that the Ardennes had "broken the backbone of Wehrmacht on the Western Front." The diarist of the Wehrmacht High Command, P. E. Schramm, later noted, "The abortive [Ardennes] offensive had made clear not only the aerial but the armored superiority of the enemy."

The Ardennes fighting had seen the last major tank-versus-tank fighting on the Western Front during the war. The U.S. Army tank force in the European theater continued to grow with the arrival of two more armored divisions and numerous smaller formations, but the Wehrmacht was obliged to shift much of its panzer force to the east when the Red Army launched its great Oder-Vistula offensive in January 1945. Many small-scale tank-versus-tank actions would continue in the months that followed, but the main threat to American tanks were German antitank guns and the dreaded panzerfaust antitank rockets.

The crew of an M7 105mm howitzer motor carriage of Battery C, 274th Armored Field Artillery Battalion, prepares to conduct a fire mission in support of Patton's Third Army near Bastogne on 1 January 1945. The side armored flap is folded down, showing the tops of the fiberboard ammunition canisters in the ammunition racks. This vehicle is also fitted with duckbill extended end connectors.

Elements of the 4th Armored Division were bivouacked in a wind-swept field outside Bastogne near Vaux-les-Rosieres in the week after Christmas, including these M4 tanks.

The first intended use for the new 4.5-inch T34 "Calliope" rocket launcher was by the 743rd Tank Battalion in support of the 30th Division's operations in the Ardennes. Here ordnance personnel are attaching the launchers to an M4 (left) and M4A3 (right).

A T34 4.5-inch rocket launcher attached to an M4 medium tank. These were not widely used in the Ardennes fighting but saw much more extensive use in the months that followed as a supplementary artillery weapon.

An M16 machine-gun motor carriage antiaircraft half-track of the 447th Anti-Aircraft Artillery Battalion is dug in near Neufchateau, Belgium, on New Year's Day during the Battle of the Bulge. This vehicle (registration number 4048604) was completed as an M13 in March 1943 with twin .50-caliber machine guns and was subsequently converted to an M16 machine-gun motor carriage with quad .50-caliber machine guns. It is still fitted with the older pattern automotive headlight. This vehicle has jerrican racks added on the winch bumper and is pattern-painted with the standard First Army black camouflage over olive drab.

The crew of a 57mm antitank gun cleans its barrel during a break in the fighting near Marche, Belgium, on 2 January. This gun belonged to an antitank company of the 334th Infantry, 84th Division, which took part in the fighting after Christmas against the 116th Panzer Division near Marche-Hotton.

An M7 105mm howitzer motor carriage of Battery B, 92nd Armored Field Artillery Battalion, 2nd Armored Division, leads the way through Monteuville, Belgium, on 2 January. This is an intermediate-production vehicle from the autumn 1942 production run featuring the E4188 one-piece transmission cover with the folding armored side panels and the D47527 vertical volute suspension. Many of the M7 105mm howitzer motor carriages of the 2nd Armored Division were fitted with stowage racks on the rear hull side like those fitted to half-tracks, and this vehicle has duckbill extended end connectors for better flotation in the muddy winter conditions.

A soldier of the 6th Armored Division inspects the hull side of a Panther on 3 January. The German tank had been knocked out in the fighting east of Bastogne. Although the Panther had formidable armor on the front, its side armor was vulnerable to the full range of American medium tank guns.

The fighting northwest of Bastogne after Christmas shattered the panzer spearheads of the Fifth Panzer Army. Here a Pz.Kpfw. IV and Panther tank of the 2nd Panzer Division are recovered by U.S. forces from the Celles pocket, where they were trapped.

The town of Noville was the scene of intense fighting during the battles for Bastogne. This is the scene after the fighting, with the streets littered with destroyed equipment, including a German StuG III assault gun in the lower left foreground, a U.S. Army M2 half-track to the right, and a U.S. M4 medium tank farther down the street.

A destroyed Jagdpanzer IV with the original PaK 39 L/48 gun, knocked out in the fighting near Bastogne.

Another Jagdpanzer IV knocked out near Bastogne. This vehicle had excellent frontal armor, but thin side armor in combination with ammunition stowage in the sponsons led to catastrophic damage when the side armor was penetrated.

A Panther Ausf. G knocked out in the fighting around Bastogne in January.

A Pz.Kpfw. IV of the 3rd Company, Panzer Regiment 33, knocked out near Recogne in January. This vehicle is fitted with the "Thoma shield" side skirts. Although often described as antibazooka shields, these side skirts were in fact added for protection against Soviet antitank rifles, which could penetrate the thinner side armor of German tanks at close ranges.

Another example of a Pz.Kpfw. IV with the Thoma shields from SS Panzer Regiment 1, knocked out near Lutrebois.

A GI inspects a knocked-out Pz.Kpfw. IV fitted with the Thoma shield mesh skirts in January.

Tanks of the 2nd Armored Division support the 84th Division during the fighting near Amonines, Belgium, on 2 January. The lead tank appears to be a composite-hull M4 fitted with the T54 metal chevron tracks with duckbill extenders. There was quite a bit of variation in the detail of the duckbills, as many were manufactured locally in shops in Belgium and France.

The Luftwaffe air attacks on New Year's Day, code-named *Bodenplatte*, led to increased vigilance by U.S. antiaircraft gunners. This is the crew of a quad M45 .50-caliber heavy machine gun turret on an M51 trailer mount of Battery C, 551st Anti-Aircraft Artillery Automatic Weapons Battalion, in Soy, Belgium, on 5 January.

An M4A3 (76mm) of the 2nd Armored Division passes a disabled German Panther Ausf. G of the 2nd SS Panzer Division along the Erezee road outside Grandmenil, Belgium, on 2 January. The Panther was one of the Sherman's most difficult opponents and was encountered far more frequently than the rare Tiger I.

M4 (105mm) assault guns of the 32nd Armored Regiment, 3rd Armored Division, conduct a fire-support mission near Trou-de-Bra on 3 January.

As snow closed in during the early winter of 1944–45, more and more American vehicles received a quick coat of whitewash like this M36 90mm gun motor carriage from one of the units of Patton's Third Army in Luxembourg during the final phase of the Battle of the Bulge. These paint jobs were often done hastily with mops or, in this case, with buckets.

Loretta II and other M4 (105mm) assault guns fire on German positions in support of the 66th Armored Regiment of the 2nd Armored Division during fighting near Amonines on 4 January. This tank is sporting a layer of sand bags for protection against German panzerfausts.

The 2nd Armored Division modified its M4 81mm mortar motor carriages by redirecting the mortar tube forward. This photo shows one of those vehicles in action on the outskirts of Amonines, Belgium, on 4 January.

After the 2nd Armored Division blunted the German advance near Celles, it took part in the counteroffensive to reduce the Bulge. Here the crew of an M4A1 (76mm) medium tank repairs the track in a wooded area near Amonines in the midst of a snow storm in early January.

The crew of an M5A1 light tank of the 2nd Armored Division cooks a meal during the fighting in the Ardennes on 5 January. By this time, the M5A1 was being replaced with the newer M24 light tank, but preference went to the cavalry squadrons rather than the light tank companies.

A whitewashed M3A1 half-track of the 21st Armored Infantry Battalion, 11th Armored Division, passes by a destroyed German Pz.Kpfw. IV in the village of Foy, Belgium, in early January.

A snow-covered Panzer IV/70 photographed in the Ardennes after the Battle of the Bulge.

The Wirbelwind 20mm Flak 38-Vierling antiaircraft tank was first issued in the summer of 1944 for defense of panzer units against air attack, and only 122 were completed. These were lost in the Ardennes.

A snow-covered M4A3E2 assault tank advances alongside a column of U.S. infantry through Liernieux, Belgium, on 2 January.

M4 (105mm) assault guns of the headquarters company of the 2nd Company, 32nd Armored Regiment, 3rd Armored Division, provide fire support during operations around Trou-de-Bra on 3 January. These resembled the usual Sherman tank, but had a 105mm howitzer in the turret instead of the usual 75mm gun to provide additional high-explosive fire support.

This Sd.Kfz. 251 half-track, probably from the 116th Panzer Division, was abandoned in Marcourt in early January. Curiously enough, the crew had substituted a captured .50-caliber Browning heavy machine gun for the usual German MG42. It is being inspected by a GI from the 4th Cavalry Group on 13 January.

A company of tanks of the 35th Tank Battalion, 4th Armored Division, along N-4 highway near Bastogne on 3 January.

In a scene evocative of the fighting in the Ardennes, an M4 tank of the 4th Armored Division moves past an entrenched .30-caliber machine-gun team of the 104th Infantry during the fighting to keep the Bastogne corridor open on 3 January.

The crew of an M15A1 machine-gun motor carriage antiaircraft half-track of Battery B, 571st Anti-Aircraft Artillery Battalion, loads 37mm ammunition near Kornelimünster, Germany, on 3 January. There was heightened interest in antiaircraft defense after months of indifference when the Luftwaffe staged its destructive but futile Operation *Bodenplatte* air offensive on New Year's Day.

A GI inspects a knocked-out Panther Ausf. G in Neffe, Belgium, on 3 January, probably from the Panzer Lehr Division, which fought for this town during the attempts to break into Bastogne.

As Kampfgruppe Peiper ran out of fuel, it gradually abandoned its tanks. One of the last to be abandoned was King Tiger 204 of the 2nd Company of schwere SS Panzer Abteilung 501 (501st SS Heavy Panzer Battalion), left behind on the road near Gue in the early morning hours of Christmas Eve after La Gleize had been abandoned. It was later driven a short distance by American troops and is seen broken down along the road near Ruy on 4 January.

The crew of an M10 tank destroyer of Company B, 629th Tank Destroyer Battalion, warms up around a fire near Manhay on 4 January. This battalion was one of a number of units taking part in the efforts to block the 2nd SS Panzer Division's retreat from Grandmenil and Manhay on 26–27 December. One M10 crew was awarded the Distinguished Service Cross posthumously for stopping a column of fourteen Panthers.

A recovery unit—including an M32 tank-recovery vehicle and a Dragon Wagon tank transporter—prepares to recover M4A3 (76mm) tanks of the 9th Armored Division that were knocked out in the fighting around Bastogne in early January.

A paratrooper of the 82nd Airborne Division leads a column of German prisoners past a disabled StuG IV assault gun in the Ardennes during the fighting around Malmedy in January.

An air force officer looks over a StuG III that was knocked out in the earlier fighting. The U.S. Army Air Force periodically sent pilots to the battlefield to get a better sense of the effectiveness of their air attacks on German ground forces.

During a snow storm, a column of paratroopers led by a tank from the 740th Tank Battalion passes by a disabled M4A1 (76mm) during the fighting near Abrefontaine on 4 January.

By January, the snow began to settle more heavily in the Ardennes. Here an M4 medium tank takes shelter alongside a road with a destroyed German Kübelwagen utility vehicle in the foreground.

An M4 high-speed tractor of Battery C, 989th Field Artillery Battalion, recovers a German 88mm FlaK 36 antiaircraft gun on 5 January. This unit operated 155mm guns in support of Patton's Third Army near Bastogne.

The crew of an M4A3 (76mm) named *Come In* of Company C, 22nd Tank Battalion, 11th Armored Division, does maintenance on its tank while bivouaced near Jodenville, Belgium, on 5 January.

The crew of an M4A3 of the 11th Armored Division loads 75mm high-explosive ammunition into its tank during a lull in the fighting near Jodenville on 5 January. Many crews had additional racks welded to the turret sides to attach their knapsacks and other kit.

This M4 tank of the 747th Tank Battalion, fitted with a E4-5 flamethrower, is seen moments after having set a barn afire near Schleiden, Germany, on 5 January.

The crew of an M7 105mm howitzer motor carriage of the 274th Armored Field Artillery Battalion sets fuzes on their 105mm ammunition prior to a fire mission near Bastogne on 5 January. This is a 1944-production M7 105mm howitzer motor carriage and gives a good view of the improved sponson stowage box on the rear of the vehicle with the new basket fit on top. It is fitted with duckbill extended end connectors for better flotation in mud and snow. This self-propelled artillery unit was one of several transferred from France during Patton's drive to relieve Bastogne.

A tank crew uses a truck to help put the track back on an M4A3 (76mm) of the 69th Tank Battalion, 6th Armored Division. This track is fitted with extended end connectors for better flotation in muddy conditions.

The snow and ice on the Belgian roads in January were hazardous even to tracked vehicles. This M36 90mm gun motor carriage tank destroyer of the 702nd Tank Destroyer Battalion, 2nd Armored Division, overturned on 5 January.

Another view of the overturned M36 tank destroyer after it has been righted with the help of a tank-recovery vehicle (out of view).

An M25 Dragon Wagon forty-ton tank transporter is used to recover a knocked-out M4 medium tank from the 4th Armored Division of Patton's Third Army outside Bastogne on 6 January. Two large penetrations can be seen on the turret, evidently from tank or antitank guns.

An M10 3-inch gun motor carriage of the 703rd Tank Destroyer Battalion, 3rd Armored Division, is stationed along a road in Belgium on 6 January. One of the crew members is trying out a pair of skis taken from a German prisoner.

On 6 January, troops of the 327th Engineer Combat Battalion were sent out into no-man's-land near Apweiler, Germany, to blow-up some knocked-out Pz.Kpfw. IV tanks to prevent the Germans from recovering them. Here they are packing one of the tanks with high explosives.

The engineers stand back while two German tanks are detonated in the background on 6 January. The engineers were supporting the 102nd Division on this assignment.

In this view, the engineers examine their handiwork, with the explosives having blown open the hull and tossed the turret aside. Curiously enough, the Pz.Kpfw. IV turret seems to have a metal panel on the roof, though it is not clear if this is debris or a unique form of appliqué armor.

An M4A3 (76mm) of the 750th Tank Battalion provides support for the 290th Infantry Regiment, 75th Division, in positions near Beffs, Belgium, on 7 January.

A GI from the 84th Division inspects an M7 105mm howitzer motor carriage knocked out near Marcoury, Belgium, during the Ardennes fighting. This is an intermediate-production vehicle with the D47527 vertical volute suspension. Curiously enough, it is still fitted with the Douglas device, one of the hedgerow cutters developed for Operation Cobra in July 1944. This particular style was most common in the 3rd Armored Division, which suggests that this vehicle may have served with one of the division's three field artillery battalions.

By early January, the snow had settled in throughout Belgium, making mobile operations all the more difficult. The 3rd Armored Division continued its efforts to reduce the northern edge of the Bulge around Manhay toward Houffalize. These two M4 medium tanks of the 33rd Armored Regiment, 3rd Armored Division, train their guns on the woods while a tank up ahead is recovered on 7 January.

This Sturmpanzer IV Brummbär was photographed by the Howell mission when it visited the Ardennes after the Battle of the Bulge.

A view from the Ardennes in the aftermath of the Battle of the Bulge by a member of the Howell mission shows an abandoned Panzer IV/70, a type widely seen during the campaign.

Another photo by the Howell mission shows an abandoned Jagdpanzer 38 to the right and an early-production Sd.Kfz. 251/17 2-centimeter flak half-track.

The crew of an M4 medium tank takes a break near the improvised gravesite of several German artillery men of the 5th Company, SS Artillery Regiment "Das Reich," near Langlir on 7 January.

Surviving King Tigers of the schwere SS Panzer Abteilung 501(501st SS Heavy Panzer Battalion) were shifted to the Bastogne front in late December 1944 to form Kampfgruppe Möbius. They took part in the futile attempts by the 1st SS Panzer Division to stop Patton's spearhead, the 4th Armored Division. At least two King Tigers were abandoned on 8 January, including this one in the outskirts of Lutremange. Alongside is a U.S. Army M5 high-speed tractor towing a 155mm howitzer.

A new M4A3E8 (76mm) of the 4th Armored Division covering the H-4 highway outside Bastogne on 8 January. The Battle of the Bulge was the first time that this new version of the M4 appeared in combat. The new horizontal volute spring suspension on this version had a wider track for better performance in snow or mud. Notice that the turret star has already been painted out.

One of the new M4A3E8 medium tanks of the 35th Tank Battalion, 4th Armored Division, during a snow storm near Bastogne on 8 January. The division was badly understrength from the fighting on the Saar front in early December before being sent to Bastogne, so it received priority for new equipment such as these tanks.

This M4 of the 747th Tank Battalion knocked out six German tanks before being knocked out itself during combat in support of the 29th Division in early January. The tank is pockmarked with small-caliber hits, probably from a 20mm antiaircraft cannon.

An M7 105mm howitzer motor carriage of the 212th Armored Field Artillery Battalion, 6th Armored Division, rests under a camouflage net while conducting fire missions near Bastogne on 8 January. During the Battle of the Bulge, this battalion set a record for 105mm battalions for firing 1,000 rounds per day. This vehicle is fairly typical of the 1944 production run, and like many vehicles in the Ardennes, it has been fitted with extended end connectors on its tracks.

An engineer maintenance company in Luxembourg used a turretless M4A3 hull fitted with an M1 dozer for support operations in Luxembourg. It is seen here on 9 January during the Battle of the Bulge. A side access door has also been added.

An M7 105mm howitzer motor carriage nicknamed *Acrobat III* of an artillery unit of Patton's Third Army prepares to fire during fighting near Morhet, Belgium, on 9 January.

An M5A1 light tank of the 4th Cavalry Recon Squadron (Mechanized) passes a knocked-out Panther tank while supporting the 84th Division in Belgium on 9 January.

An M2A1 half-track of the 6th Armored Division on the outskirts of Bastogne on 9 January. This version of the half-track was characterized by an added machine-gun pulpit on the right side of the vehicle.

A battery of M7 105mm howitzer motor carriages of the 2nd Armored Division moves forward near Samree on 10 January. The lead vehicle is a November 1942–production vehicle, one of the first fitted with the armored side flaps.

Kathleen, an M4A3 (76mm) of Company B, 41st Tank Battalion, receives a coat of whitewash camouflage on 10 January while bivouacked in Bereneux, Belgium.

A column from the 75th Division supported by tanks of the 750th Tank Battalion moves forward near Basse Bodeux, Belgium, on 10 January to relieve the 82nd Airborne Division.

Another view of the 75th Division column with an M4A3 tank of the 750th Tank Battalion. This tank has the duckbill extenders on its track and appears to have sand-bag armor on the glacis plate as well.

An M4A1 (76mm) medium tank of the 774th Tank Battalion accompanies troops of the 83rd Division as they pass through Bihain, Belgium, on 11 January.

The Battle of the Bulge was the debut for the new M4A3 with the horizontal volute spring suspension; at the time, the tankers called it the "M4A3 (76mm) with 23-inch track" and later the M4A3E8. One of the first units into Bastogne was Company B, 37th Tank Battalion, 4th Armored Division, led by Capt. James Leach. This is his replacement tank, *Block Buster 3rd*.

A close-up of the side of Leach's M4A3E8, with the captain pointing at the tank's name. This was the third Sherman operated by the crew since 1944.

An M4A1 (76mm) moves along a snow-covered road near Odeigne, Belgium, on 11 January. It has extended end connectors fitted to the track.

An officer inspects an M4A1 (76mm) of the 3rd Armored Division that suffered an antitank gun hit on the right hull side. The remnants of the hedgerow cutter from the Normandy campaign are still evident on the lower transmission cover.

Another knocked-out M4A1 (76mm) of the 3rd Armored Division seen in Cherein, Belgium, on 17 January.

This Sd.Kfz. 251/6 command post half-track was set on fire after its capture near Jodenville by American combat engineers because of the large amount of munitions it was carrying. It may have been part of the Panzer Lehr Division.

On occasion, captured German artillery was employed if ammunition was available. Here M4 high-speed tractors are towing a pair of German 88mm PaK 43/41 heavy antitank guns while supporting operations by the 90th Division in Luxembourg on 11 January. These massive guns were appropriately nicknamed the *Scheunentor* ("barn door") by their German crews because of their massive size.

This King Tiger was knocked out in fighting with the 6th Armored Division near Wardin during the Battle of the Bulge and was photographed on 12 January.

During the later phases of the Battle of the Bulge, many tanks were camouflage-painted with lime whitewash. This was not a particularly delicate procedure, as is evident from the scene of a 7th Armored Division tanker painting his M4 near Xhorie, Belgium, on 11 January.

The crew of an M4A1 (76mm) of the 741st Tank Battalion cleans the bore of its tank's 76mm gun on 11 January while supporting the 2nd Infantry Division.

An M4A3 (76mm) leads a column from the 712th Tank Battalion during operations near Bavigne, Luxembourg, on 12 January. It is fitted with T48 rubber chevron track with duckbill extenders.

An M4 medium tank being used for forward observers of the 492nd Field Artillery moves toward Longchamps on 13 January. The road sign reads "Vers Bastogne"—toward Bastogne.

A Panther Ausf. G (tactical number 121) of the 9th Panzer Division, knocked out by a 57mm antitank gun during the fighting for Langlir to the northeast of Houffalize on 13 January. Although the 57mm antitank gun was ineffective against the Panther's thick frontal armor, it could penetrate the side armor. Note the penetration in the turret side in the lower rear corner of the tactical number. The 9th Panzer Division typically painted its tactical numbers in plain white on the rear side of the turret.

An M36 90mm gun motor carriage of the 703rd Tank Destroyer Battalion, 3rd Armored Division, passes by a derelict Pz.Kpfw. IV of Panzer Abteilung 115 (115th Panzer Battalion), 15th Panzergrenadier Division, south of Langlir on 13 January.

The crew of an M7 105mm howitzer motor carriage of the 3rd Armored Division load ammunition during a fire mission in Belgium. The 105mm howitzer ammunition came packed in fiberboard tubes, as can be seen in the arms of the soldier lifting to round to the cannoneer on the vehicle.

An M32B1 tank-recovery vehicle of Company C, 603rd Tank Destroyer Battalion, attached at the time to the 6th Armored Division, is seen in operation near Bastogne on 14 January during the Battle of the Bulge. The M32B1 was an armored recovery vehicle based on the hull of the M4A1 tank, fitted with a new turret, a winch, and an A-frame crane.

A pair of M8 armored cars moves out on a scouting mission on 14 January. They are part of C Troop, 2nd Cavalry Squadron, which was supporting the 4th Infantry Division in the Bastogne area at the time. The lead vehicle has been whitewashed, leaving the white Allied star in an olive-drab circle.

The streets of Houffalize were littered with abandoned equipment following the retreat of the 116th Panzer Division on 14 January. One of the more unusual items was this old Pz.Kpfw. III, which was being used as a command tank.

Another view of the same street later in January showing one of the abandoned Pz.Kpfw. III tanks in Houffalize.

A view of the fields outside Houffalize after the fighting, littered with the burnt-out carcasses of several Panther tanks.

The crews of two M4A3 (76mm)'s of the 771st Tank Battalion peer off into the distance at a German artillery strike on the outskirts of Berismenil, Belgium, on 14 January while supporting the 84th Division.

M31 tank-recovery vehicles from the 3rd Company, 66th Armored Regiment, try to extract a bogged M4 of the 2nd Armored Division near Les Tailles, Belgium, on 14 January. The M31 nearest the camera was named *Invader*.

An M4A3 (76mm) of the 15th Tank Battalion, 6th Armored Division, crunches through a pine woods outside Benonchamps, Belgium, on 14 January.

An M36 90mm gun motor carriage tank destroyer of the 703rd Tank Destroyer Battalion, 3rd Armored Division, is parked in an ambush position in a pine woods on 14 January.

An M4A3 (76mm) of the 42nd Tank Battalion, 11th Armored Division, passes by an abandoned German Pz.Kpfw. IV tank along the Houffalize road outside Bastogne on 15 January. The 11th Armored Division had been one of the units used to widen the corridor into Bastogne at the end of December; it then took part in efforts to break out of the encirclement on the eastern side of the town.

A pair of M5A1's of Company D, 37th Tank Battalion, 4th Armored Division, returns to the battalion's base camp outside Bastogne on 14 January.

Crew members of the M4A3 (76mm) command tank of Capt. John Megglesin of the 42nd Tank Battalion, 11th Armored Division, cross their fingers for luck. This new tank was the third they had been issued in two weeks of fighting. The two previous tanks had been knocked out, fortunately without the loss of a single crewman. It was a grim statistic that on average, one crewman was killed every time a Sherman was knocked out.

Troops of the intelligence and reconnaissance platoon of the 63rd Armored Infantry Battalion, 11th Armored Division, bring in a couple of Wehrmacht prisoners near Longchamps on 15 January.

American infantry moves up north of Bastogne near Compogne, Belgium, on 15 January, past a disabled Flakpanzer IV Wirbelwind. This antiaircraft version of the Pz.Kpfw. IV tank was armed with a four-barrel 20mm FlaK 38 antiaircraft cannon.

An M4A1 medium tank of the 743rd Tank Battalion fitted with an M1 dozer blade leads a column through Malmedy to help clear away snow. The second tank in the column is one of the rare M4A3E2 Jumbo assault tanks. At the time, this battalion was supporting the 38th Division in efforts to reduce the Bulge.

A rare view of a Sherman unit deployed for combat. A company of tanks from the 11th Armored Division awaits orders to attack German positions in the town of Compogne, Belgium, on 15 January.

An M2A1 half-track car towing an M3 37mm antitank gun crosses a bridge that was recently erected by troops of the 49th Combat Engineer Battalion (seen in the foreground) on 15 January near the town of Houffalize. Some of units in the "heavy" armored divisions still had these old 37mm antitank guns under the 1942 table of organization and kept them for additional firepower even after being issued the newer 57mm antitank gun.

An M4 of the 10th Armored Division knocked out near Neffe, Belgium, during the fighting around Bastogne, photographed on 15 January.

As the battle decreased in intensity, efforts increased to recover many of the tanks damaged and destroyed during the earlier fighting. Here a crew attempts to recover a burned-out composite-hull M4 of the 69th Tank Battalion, 6th Armored Division, near Wardin, Belgium, in mid-January.

A curious photo showing the view from behind a German 75mm PaK 40 antitank gun that knocked out the M3 half-track of the 6th Armored Division seen in the foreground on 16 January near Wardin, Belgium. The German antitank gun was subsequently put out of action by the accompanying armored infantry.

This pair of Shermans from the 15th Tank Battalion, 6th Armored Division, was knocked out near Longvilly during efforts to break out of the Bastogne encirclement.

This M4 composite-hull medium tank is the one on the right in the photo above. Carrying tactical number 50, it also displays the battalion's tactical marking on the rear side—a wolf's head on a tricolor Armored Force triangle, superimposed on a white square.

This close-up of the M4 (tactical number 73) on the left in the top photo shows the results of a massive internal ammunition explosion that has peeled the right side armor back and blown the turret off the turret race.

The crewman of an M31 tank-recovery vehicle of the 3rd Armored Division survived a near miss.

An M4A3 of Company C, 15th Tank Battalion, 6th Armored Division, during the push to the northeast of Bastogne in mid-January. This tank, named *Cougar*, carries tactical number 77, also its radio call sign. This attack was part of a broader push by Patton's Third Army from Bastogne toward "Skyline Drive" at the northern eastern end of the Bulge.

The crew of an M4 (105mm) assault gun (tactical number 15) of HQ Company, 15th Tank Battalion, 6th Armored Division, near Trois Vierge, Luxembourg, warms up over a fire while waiting for another support mission on 24 January. These tanks were used to provide indirect fire support for the regular medium tanks of the battalion; expended casings can be seen scattered around the tank.

A view of a neighboring M4 (105mm) assault gun from HQ Company of the 15th Tank Battalion, 6th Armored Division, during the fighting to link up with the First Army in mid-January.

A column of half-tracks from the 6th Armored Division moves along a snow-covered tree line during the attempts to push out of Bastogne in late January.

An M4 of the 68th Tank Battalion, 6th Armored Division, carries infantry forward during the fighting in mid-January. Its tactical number is 47, and it carries the white triangle typical of this battalion.

Another 6th Armored Division Sherman casualty, this M4 was knocked out by a German panzerfaust or panzerschreck in Mageret, Belgium, during January.

A perennial chore for tankers: repairing damaged track. This 6th Armored Division crew is seen repairing its track on the outskirts of Bastogne on 15 January.

An abandoned King Tiger of SS schwere Panzer Abteilung 501 (501st SS Heavy Panzer Battalion) is inspected by troops of the 82nd Airborne Division in the Ambleve Valley in January.

Another abandoned King Tiger of the 501 is inspected by troops of the 82nd Airborne.

Patton's Third Army linked up with the First Army along the Ourthe River on 16 January, with troops of the 84th Division shaking hands with an M8 armored car crew from the 11th Armored Division. This linked up both the eastern and western shoulders of the Bulge for the first time.

M4 (105mm) assault guns of HQ Company, 774th Tank Battalion, provide fire support for the 75th Infantry Division on 16 January.

An M4A3 (76mm) of the 750th Tank Battalion moves into Salmchateau in support of the 75th Division on 16 January. The tank has been thoroughly whitewashed; on the back deck is a long fluorescent orange air-identity panel to prevent strafing by Allied aircraft.

Tanks of Company H, 66th Armored Regiment, 2nd Armored Division, move forward prior to the operation from Houffalize on 16 January. The composite-hull M4 nearer the camera is named *Harm* while the M4A3 (76mm) is named *Homme de Guerre* (*Man of War*).

An intelligence and reconnaissance platoon from the 60th Infantry, 9th Division, developed this improvised mounting for a pair of 2.35-inch bazookas using the normal .50-caliber heavy machine gun pedestal in a jeep. This vehicle was photographed in Belgium on 16 January.

This other view of the bazooka-armed jeep from a 60th Infantry intelligence and reconnaissance platoon also shows how the crew has added a partial armored shield around the front of the vehicle from plate steel.

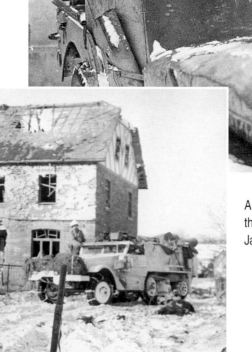

A whitewashed M2 half-track passes through the ruins of Faymonville on 16 January after its capture.

An M8 armored car of the 4th Cavalry Squadron, 4th Cavalry Group, in Borzee, Germany, toward the end of the campaign on 16 January. This cavalry unit had been attached to the 2nd Armored Division for much of the fighting in Belgium, and the 4th Squadron was often used to screen between CCA and CCB. This M8 shows the wear and tear of combat; it is missing its side skirts and festooned with crew gear. It has been given a hasty camouflage of whitewash and is fitted with tire chains to help negotiate the muddy and icy roads.

On 16 January, Faymonville fell to the U.S. 1st Infantry Division. Among the equipment abandoned in the town by the 3rd Fallschirmjäger (Paratroop) Division was this M8 armored car. It is quite likely that this was one of the armored cars of the 14th Cavalry Group captured during the fighting in the Losheim Gap at the start of the Ardennes offensive.

M32B1 tank-recovery vehicles of Company B, 738th Tank Battalion (Special Mine Exploder, or SMX) are used to attach a T1E1 mine-roller assembly near Faymonville, Belgium, on 16 January.

An M32B1 with T1E1 Earthworm of Company B, 738th Tank Battalion (SMX), near Faymonville on 16 January during the Battle of the Bulge, with an M3A1 half-track to the left.

An M32B1 of Company B, 738th Tank Battalion (SMX), pushes a T1E1 Earthworm mine exploder down a road near Faymonville on 16 January.

A T1E1 Earthworm is pushed by an M32B1 of the 738th Tank Battalion (SMX) in front of a column from the 2nd Armored Division near Houffalize on 16 January.

A T1E3 Aunt Jemima of the 738th Tank Battalion (SMX) in action on a road near an improvised Wehrmacht cemetery in Recht, Belgium, in mid-January. This provides a good view of the pusher plate at the rear of the tank, which was designed to permit another tank to get behind the mine-roller tank and give it a push if stuck.

A task force of M36's from the 702nd Tank Destroyer Battalion (on the left) and M4 medium tanks of the 66th Armored Regiment of the 2nd Armored Division prepare for an attack on Houffalize on 16 January. During the Ardennes fighting, it was common to attach a few M36 tank destroyers to tank battalions since their 90mm gun was the only sure way to deal with German heavy tanks.

M4 medium tanks followed by an M5A1 light tank of Company D, 42nd Tank Battalion, 11th Armored Division, push toward Mabompre, Belgium, on 16 January.

A number of Sd.Kfz. 251 half-tracks were captured by the U.S. Ninth Army north of the Ardennes, and they were often pressed into service if still serviceable. This one is being used by the 497th Medical Detachment on 17 January after being repainted olive drab and marked with Red Cross insignia and a U.S. registration number.

American infantry units defended themselves against tank attack using the 57mm antitank gun, a license copy of the British 6-pounder. It was obsolete by 1944, though it could knock out a Panther tank from the side or rear. This is a 57mm gun of the 333rd Anti-Tank Company, 83rd Division, near Bovigny on 17 January.

Some idea of the intensity of the fighting beyond Bastogne is evident in this photo. The M4A3 from the 6th Armored Division has been knocked out at close range by a panzerfaust from the crew of the Sd.Kfz. 251 half-track that had taken refuge in the neighboring church on 17 January. The half-track has Red Cross markings like an ambulance.

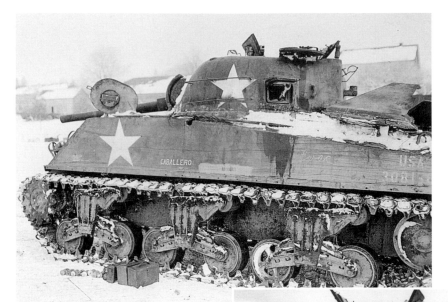

Cabellero, an M4A3 medium tank of the 69th Tank Battalion, 6th Armored Division, is recovered after the fighting to push out of Bastogne near Longvilly in mid-January. It has taken a hit on the upper hull side immediately above the vehicle name. This is the late-production version of the 75mm gun tank with wet ammunition stowage, the simplified forty-seven-degree hull front, and the modernized turret with a loader's hatch.

Another view of *Caballero* being recovered near Longvilly in late January. A hit can be seen to the immediate left of the vehicle name on the side.

A Panther Ausf. G tank (tactical number 412) from the 9th Panzer Division, knocked out near the village church in Sterpigny, Belgium, to the south of Langlir. This tank took part in attempts by the 9th Panzer Division to rebuff the advance of the 3rd Armored Division on 17 January to the northeast of Houffalize. It was knocked out by a trio of tank destroyers of the 703rd Tank Destroyer Battalion, which pumped three rounds into the rear engine compartment.

This German 10.5cm leFH 18 howitzer, being towed by a Maultier half-track truck, was abandoned near Wardin to the southeast of Bastogne during the January retreat. This was the standard divisional field gun of the Wehrmacht.

An M4A3 (76mm) of Company C, 774th Tank Battalion, passes by a disabled Panther in the forest near Bovigny on 17 January while supporting the 83rd Division during the drive to seal the Bulge.

Another Sherman killer put out of action. Some GIs sit on a 75mm PaK 40 anti-tank gun, the Sherman's main foe for much of the fighting in Europe. The breech has been completely sheared off, suggesting that the Germans detonated an explosive charge in the barrel before abandoning the gun.

While Company C was moving through the Bovigny forest, Company A of the 774th was whitewashing its tanks in Joubieval on 17 January to help camouflage them in the snow.

The 117th Infantry Regiment, 30th Division, moved across the Ambleve River along the Pont-Recht road on 17 January during the attack toward St. Vith. The 2nd Battalion of the 117th was supported by this M4A3E2 Jumbo assault tank of the 743rd Tank Battalion, protected by sand bags along its side as well as its added armor.

Company I, 16th Infantry, 1st Infantry Division, rides into combat on the back of an M4A3 tank of the 745th Tank Battalion during the attack in the snow-covered town of Schopen, Belgium, in the final phase of the Battle of the Bulge.

Kampfgruppe Peiper left behind thirty-nine tanks, seventy half-tracks, and thirty other vehicles in La Gleize when they finally abandoned the town on 24 December. An intelligence and reconnaissance platoon from the 82nd Airborne Division later decided to use some of the tanks to test the penetration capabilities of the bazooka. To the left is a derelict Panther, while down in the gully is the target of the bazooka team, a King Tiger from schwere SS Panzer Abteilung 501 (501st SS Heavy Panzer Battalion).

Crewmen of an M4A1 (76mm) add foliage to their tank in an effort to improve its camouflage near Kiewelbach, Luxembourg, on 18 January. This tank is fitted with metal chevron track and duckbill end extenders.

A depot-fresh M4A3E8 at the Charmes, France, depot of the 98th Ordnance Company (Tank-HM) prior to being shipped to American tank units in Belgium. The ordnance depots often painted the tanks with official markings, but when issued to the troops, the conspicuous white stars would usually be painted over with olive drab or black paint. The only star usually left intact was the one on the engine deck.

A view inside the turret of an M4A3E8 from the commander's station looking down toward the gunner's station, with the 76mm gun to the left. The gun was shrouded with a protective cage to prevent the crew from being injured when the gun recoiled.

Another view of a brand-new M4A3E8 at the Charmes depot prior to being shipped to tank units in the Ardennes.

A view down through the Sherman's loader's hatch on the left side of the turret. The tanker is reloading ammunition in the stowage racks in the floor.

The first of the new M24 light tanks went into combat with the 740th Tank Battalion in support of the 82nd Airborne Division against Kampfgruppe Peiper in December. The 740th arrived in Belgium in December without any tanks and was told to equip itself with anything it could find. This M24 was located on a shipment going to a cavalry squadron, leading to its unofficial combat debut. Here it is seen being looked over by curious troops of the 82nd Airborne on 19 January in Nonceveux, Belgium.

Another view of the M24 above from the rear.

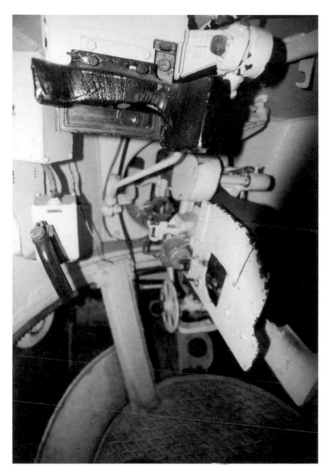

Left: One idea of the relative sophistication of the new M24 compared to the older M5A1 can be seen in the interior layout. This is the very simple interior of an M5A1 looking forward from the gunner's seat on the left side of the turret at the fire controls. Right: In comparison, this is the view from the gunner's seat in the M24 showing the much more elaborate fire controls and sighting devices.

The new M24 light tank was so novel in layout that examples were dispatched to many units along the front for demonstrations and recognition training. The M24 was nicknamed the "Panther Pup" by some GIs who thought it looked like a smaller version of the German tank. This example is being demonstrated to the 99th Division in early 1945. The M24 tended to carry more national stars than other tanks, largely because of recognition concerns.

Wind-driven snow completely covers the side of an M15A1 combination gun motor carriage of the 778th Anti-Aircraft Artillery Battalion attached to the 3rd Armored Division near Bastogne on 19 January.

Alley Oop II, one of the new M24 light tanks, during actions on 14 January.

A snow-covered M10 3-inch gun motor carriage of the 629th Tank Destroyer Battalion passes by a monument to veterans of World War I in the town of Bovigny, Belgium, while supporting operations by the 329th Regiment, 83rd Infantry Division, on 20 January.

M3A1 half-tracks of the 44th Armored Infantry, 6th Armored Division, rendezvous in a field outside Mageret, Belgium, on 20 January. All the vehicles have whitewash camouflage, and most have their canvas tarps over the troop compartment to better protect the infantry squads inside from the cold weather.

A view of an M10 3-inch gun motor carriage of the 629th Tank Destroyer Battalion later on 20 January while the crew warms up near a fire with troops of the 331st Infantry Regiment near Courtil, Belgium.

Refueling in the field was usually done using jerricans, not specialized refueling trucks. Here an M4 tank of the 7th Armored Division near Weims, Belgium, is refueled from a two-and-a-half-ton truck on 20 January.

A column of white-washed M4A3 (76mm) tanks of Combat Command A, 7th Armored Division, moves forward on 20 January from Edenbach toward St. Vith.

A column of infantry from the 90th Division supported by half-tracks from the 6th Armored Division move forward near Lullange, Luxembourg, on 22 January.

Several tanks of Combat Command A, 7th Armored Division, prepare for a night defensive position in the fields near Weims, Belgium, in the late afternoon of 20 January. The tank in the center of the image is an M4 (105mm) assault gun.

A formation of tanks of the 7th Armored Division on the outskirts of Hunnage on 23 January, with a pair of M5A1 light tanks to the rear.

A snow-camouflaged M4A3 of the 750th Tank Battalion provides support to an advance by the 75th Infantry Division near St. Vith on 23 January. This tank appears to have a layer of cement armor covering the glacis plate instead of the more common sandbag armor.

An M4A3 (76mm) tank of the 7th Armored Division supports the 23rd Armored Infantry Battalion during the capture of the town of Hunnage on the way to St. Vith on 23 January.

Troops of the 7th Armored Division walk past a disabled StuG III assault gun in the outskirts of St. Vith on 23 January.

GIs of Company C, 23rd Armored Infantry Battalion, 7th Armored Division, wait for orders in the streets of St. Vith, scene of some of the most intense fighting in the initial stages of the Battle of the Bulge in December. The M4A3 in the background has been camouflaged with temporary whitewash.

The following day, the 23rd Armored Infantry Battalion, 7th Armored Division, moved out of St. Vith to capture the small town of Wallerode to the northeast. This Jagdpanzer 38(t) Hetzer was knocked out during the fighting. The Hetzer was widely used in Volksgrenadier divisions in lieu of the StuG III, but its thin side armor made it vulnerable, as is so evident here. The combat photographer who shot this scene was killed moments later during the fighting in Wallerode.

An M5A1 from the 7th Armored Division provides support for a column of infantry from the 509th Parachute Infantry near St. Vith on 24 January.

Snow-covered M4 medium tanks of the 40th Tank Battalion, 7th Armored Division, in the outskirts of St. Vith on 24 January. The tank in the foreground has its hull side covered in a camouflage net.

Although the King Tiger was used extensively in the Ardennes, there were only a handful of the older Tiger I tanks in action in Belgium, belonging to schwere Panzerkompanie "Hummel" (Heavy Panzer Company "Hummel"), which was attached to schwere Panzer Abteilung 506 (506th Heavy Panzer Battalion) as its 4th Company. At the start of the campaign, "Hummel" had eight Tiger I's while the 506 had forty-seven King Tigers. This particular tank was abandoned near Oberwampach, Luxembourg, where it was photographed on 21 January.

The 773rd Tank Destroyer Battalion was one of the most successful units of its type and was credited with destroying 103 German tanks by the end of the Ardennes campaign. The crew of this M10, seen near Benonchamps on 21 January, was credited with five German tanks knocked out during a German counterattack near Oberwampach during the fighting around Bastogne.

Lt. O. Odens, a field artillery forward observer, stands outside his M4 medium tank while talking over the radio with other units from the 7th Armored Division during operations near St. Vith on 25 January. The forward observers were assigned to forward tank units to help provide accurate artillery support during combat operations

By the end of January, the Belgian countryside was deep in snow. Here a 2nd Armored Division column of whitewashed tanks led by a sandbagged M4 (76mm) tank moves through Eisenne, Belgium, on the way to the front on 21 January.

An M18 76mm gun motor carriage of the 2nd Armored Division comes skidding around a curve near Fisenne, Belgium, on 21 January. The icy roads in Belgium were a particular problem to rubber-tracked vehicles; the steel tracks usually used on the M18 provided better traction.

An armored infantry battalion in M3A1 half-tracks moves up through a snow-covered pine woods near Born, Belgium, on 21 January.

An M10 3-inch gun motor carriage tank destroyer passes through a destroyed village.

American units sometimes made use of captured German equipment. In this case, Company L, 3rd Battalion, 16th Infantry, 1st Infantry Division, has adopted this Sd.Kfz. 251/7 combat engineer half-track after prominently re-marking it with white stars. It still carries its Wehrmacht license plate and is being used to carry supplies near Schoppen, Belgium, on 22 January.

An abandoned Pz.Kpfw. IV tank on the Luxembourg frontier in late January. The ground is littered with crew effects, which suggests the crew left in a hurry.

An M4A3E2 assault tank of the 737th Tank Battalion advances through Gralingen, Luxembourg, on 22 January during the final phase of the Battle of the Bulge. Its surfaces are covered with Sommerfield matting, which was attached to the tank by engineer units to permit the attachment of foliage camouflage.

An M5A1 of the 17th Cavalry in a fixed defensive position in Germany on 22 January during the fighting along the Roer. It is still fitted with a Richardson device, a variation of the Culin hedgerow cutter developed by the 3rd Armored Division. A large stowage rack has been added to the turret rear.

This Flakpanzer IV Wirbelwind was abandoned in Patton's Third Army sector near Bastogne, where it was photographed on 23 January under a cover of snow and communication wire. It was earmarked for shipment back to the United States for technical evaluation.

An M29 utility vehicle is used to deliver supplies to a tank destroyer battalion near Schoppen on 23 January. These small tracked carriers were popular in the Ardennes because of their good flotation on snow.

An M8 75mm howitzer motor carriage has its engine replaced by personnel of the 133rd Ordnance Maintenance Battalion near Vaux-les-Rosieres, Belgium, on 23 January. The M8 75mm howitzer motor carriage, like the M5A1 light tank on which it was based, was powered by two Cadillac automotive engines.

A tanker of the 42nd Tank Battalion, 11th Armored Division, uses a lull in the fighting near Steinbach, Belgium, to mend his clothes on a sewing machine in front of his M4A3 tank.

Infantry from the 30th Division pass a knocked-out StuG III assault gun near Nieder Emmeiser on 23 January.

On 24 January, artillery supporting a 1st Infantry Division attack on Ambleve, Belgium, knocked this StuG IV assault gun on its side. This was a less common version of the assault gun, based on the Pz.Kpfw. IV chassis instead of the Pz.Kpfw. III chassis.

An M7 105mm howitzer motor carriage of the 342nd Armored Field Artillery Battalion opens fire near Ludweiller, Germany, on 24 January. This was one of a number of nondivisional field artillery battalions that was converted to self-propelled howitzers in 1943.

An M4A3 tank of the 745th Tank Battalion, supporting the 16th Infantry, 1st Infantry Division, during the fighting near Amel, Belgium, on 24 January.

Infantry of the 83rd Division move through Bihain on 24 January while supported by tanks from the 774th Tank Battalion, with an M4A1 (76mm) evident in this view.

On 22–25 January, German forces on the Luxembourg-German frontier attempted to withdraw but were hit by repeated air attacks by the XIX Tactical Air Command, including this Panther knocked out near Marnach.

A Panther Ausf. G (tactical number 301) from the 2nd Panzer Division abandoned near Clervaux, Luxembourg, because of engine problems when the town was retaken by the 26th Infantry Division on 25 January. Like most of the Panthers serving during the campaign, this is a fairly new vehicle, produced no earlier than October 1944 judging from the late-style self-cleaning idler wheels. It also features the late flame dampers on the exhaust and the crew compartment heater.

A GI examines some of the gear from an abandoned Sd.Kfz. 251/7 half-track. This was the standard engineer version of the German half-track.

The debris of war still litters the streets of Clervaux in February after the end of the battle. A StuG III from the 2nd Panzer Division has been pushed off the road, as has an M4A3 (76mm) of the 707th Tank Battalion, knocked out during the intense fighting in December during the Fifth Panzer Army's attack toward neighboring Bastogne.

A Daimler-Benz DB 10 twelve-ton Zugkraftwagen of the 2nd Panzer Division lies disabled in the streets of Marnach, Luxembourg, following the recapture of the town by the 26th Infantry Division on 25 January. This vehicle was used in panzer divisions to tow heavy artillery.

German units made use of captured equipment when possible, especially the Seventh Army, which was short of tanks. This M4A3 medium tank was knocked out by the U.S. 10th Armored Division at the end of January during the fighting in Luxembourg, losing its turret. The American white stars on the side had been painted out; barely evident on the bow is a German cross.

An M8 armored car near the German frontier on 26 January. The sign on the road side in German forbids halting and parking, a regulation intended to minimize the threat of Allied air attack. Three of the crew here wear British armored crewmen helmets.

An M4A1 (76mm) of the 701st Tank Battalion is serviced in a small town in Belgium before moving out in support of the 102nd Infantry Division's advance on 25 January.

It was rare to see American and British tanks together on the same mission. The exception was along the border of the U.S. Ninth Army and the British 21st Army Group, where the two allies met. Here an American M4 can be seen near a British Churchill during a joint attack against the town of Brachelen on 26 January.

Troops help push a medical jeep out of the snow and slush while evacuating casualties from the 53rd Armored Infantry Battalion, 4th Armored Division, near Asch, Luxembourg, on 26 January; an M8 light armored car is evident in the background.

A pair of knocked-out M4A3 (76mm), probably from the 9th Armored Division, during the clean-up in the wake of the Battle of the Bulge. They have the characteristic Sommerfield matting welded to the hull side for attaching foliage camouflage.

The gun commander waits for orders to fire over his field telephone as the crew loads another round on their M7 105mm howitzer motor carriage during a fire mission by the 398th Armored Field Artillery Battalion, 8th Armored Division, near Wochern, Germany, on 27 January.

Paratroopers of the 504th Parachute Infantry Regiment, 82nd Airborne Division, are supported by a company of tanks from the 740th Tank Battalion during snowy weather near Herresbach, Belgium, on 28 January.

Some of the paratroopers get a ride aboard an M4A3 (76mm) of the 740th Tank Battalion during operations near Herresbach on 28 January.

The advance on the 504th Parachute Infantry Regiment outside Herresbach on 28 January continues with troops being helped forward on the tanks of the 740th Tank Battalion.

An M29 utility vehicle is used as an ambulance to move casualties of the 82nd Airborne Division near Herresbach on 29 January.

An M29 utility vehicle is being used to evacuate casualties from the 18th Infantry, 1st Division, near Herscheid, Belgium, on 28 January. As is evident from the markings, these vehicles were often assigned to ordnance units and then used to form a pool of utility vehicles to serve as ambulances during major engagements. The camouflage is the official pattern for such vehicles.

Another M29 utility vehicle being used as an ambulance in support of the 78th Division at the end of January. The M29 was widely used as an ambulance since the normal ambulances—converted jeeps—could not negotiate the icy, snow-covered roads.

An M7 105mm howitzer motor carriage of the VIII Corps towing an M10 ammunition trailer passes through Bastogne on the way to the Ardennes front on 28 January.

A 105mm howitzer of the 915th Field Artillery Battalion in winter camouflage provides fire support near Winterspelt, Germany, on 7 February.

Sometimes even the most powerful vehicle needs a good tug. The crew of this M4 high-speed tractor towing a 155mm howitzer is extending the tow cable from the front winch to an unseen vehicle in the foreground to help extract it from a deep patch of snow or ice. This vehicle belonged to the 809th Field Artillery Battalion and is seen near Nederscheid, Belgium, on 30 January.

A very serious snow plow! This M4A3 dozer tank of the 745th Tank Battalion supporting the 1st Infantry Division was being used to clear roads near Muringen, Belgium, on 30 January.

Another example of a captured M4A3 medium tank in use by German Seventh Army troops in the Ardennes, this time near Dasburg, the crossing point between Luxembourg and Germany. This particular one was knocked out by an air strike in February; it lost its turret to an internal ammunition explosion. It was later recovered by the 6th Armored Division.

A pair of Sd.Kfz. 251 Ausf. D half-tracks abandoned off the side of a road near Dasburg and captured by the 6th Armored Division during the fighting along the Our River.

The new M24 light tank was earmarked for mechanized cavalry squadrons, which had previously relied on the inadequate M5A1 light tank. The badly mauled 14th Cavalry Group was rebuilt in Belgium following the Ardennes campaign. Its M5A1 light tanks were replaced with the much-improved M24 Chaffee light tank, seen here with the 18th Cavalry Squadron at Petit Tier, Belgium, on 3 February.

The novel appearance of the M24 prompted the U.S. Army to send examples around the front to acquaint the troops with the new type for fear that it would be mistaken as a German tank. Here an ordnance team explains the new tank to members of the 39th Infantry near Kalterdern, Germany, on 31 January.

Destroyed equipment littered the Belgian countryside for years after the fighting. This Panther had been destroyed by an internal ammunition explosion in the village of Rachamps, Belgium, and some local cows use it for shelter in March 1945.

The shattered remains of an M3A1 half-track in the wake of the Battle of the Bulge.

A StuG III assault gun lies abandoned in a shattered Ardennes village near the Luxembourg frontier. This is a late-production version with the *Saukopf* ("pig's head") gun mantlet.

CHAPTER 2

Operation Nordwind

WHILE THE BATTLE OF THE BULGE is familiar enough to have been the subject of Hollywood movies, the other German winter offensive in the western theater remains obscure, and Gen. Omar Bradley's 12th Army Group has received far more attention than Gen. Jacob Devers's smaller 6th Army Group farther south in Alsace. In the waning hours of New Year's Eve 1944, the Wehrmacht launched Operation Nordwind in Alsace. This was a desperate attempt to exploit the disruptions caused by the Ardennes offensive farther north in Belgium. After Patton's Third Army shifted two of its corps to relieve Bastogne, Gen. Alexander Patch's neighboring Seventh Army was forced to extend its front lines to cover the gap. The weak American defenses in Alsace presented the Wehrmacht with a rare opportunity to mass its forces.

Although the Nordwind offensive was intended to be a complementary attack to the Ardennes attack, by the time it started in early January, the fate of the Ardennes battle had already been decided. The failure of that offensive convinced Hitler that some new tactic had to be employed when dealing with the Allies. Instead of a single large offensive, Hitler decided to launch a series of smaller, sequential offensives. As a result, some German command-

ers called the Alsace campaign the "Sylwester offensives" after the Central European name for the New Year's Eve celebrations.

The initial Nordwind offensive emanated out of the fortified border city of Bitche but made little progress in the face of stiff American resistance. In view of the failure of the initial Nordwind offensive around Bitche, Hitler shifted the focus of the Alsace operation farther east toward Hagenau, attempting to link up the two attack forces and push the U.S. Army away from the Rhine. This led to a series of extremely violent tank battles in the middle of January around the towns of Hatten-Rittershoffen and Herrlisheim that exhausted both sides. An experienced German panzer commander later called these winter battles the fiercest ever fought on the Western Front. These involved the U.S. 12th and 14th Armored Divisions as well as Waffen SS panzer divisions.

By the time the Red Army launched its winter offensive into central Germany on 14 January, the Wehrmacht had exhausted its potential in Alsace. Panzer units were transferred to the Russian front, and German infantry units began to take up defensive positions. It was time for Devers's 6th Army Group to smash the Wehrmacht on the western bank of the Rhine. The largest pocket of German troops was trapped around Colmar. The French First Army did not have the strength to do it quickly, so in late January, additional American divisions were moved into Alsace from the Ardennes. In two weeks of fierce winter fighting, the German Nineteenth Army was decisively defeated, and the survivors of the Colmar pocket retreated over the Rhine. The German Sylwester offensives were the death rattle of the Wehrmacht in the west. After these ill-conceived attacks, the Wehrmacht would never again be able to conduct anything but local counterattacks in the west because all of its operational reserves had been spent or shipped off to the east.

German Army Group G had very little armor support in the initial phases of Operation Nordwind, with the largest concentration being the StuG III assault guns of the 17th SS Panzergrenadier Division. This particular photo was found by American troops in Colmar after Nordwind and shows one of the StuG III assault guns at the start of the attacks.

Because of the significant number of Maginot Line fortifications in the Nordwind operations zone, the German First Army was allotted two companies of flamethrower tanks equipped with the new Flammpanzer 38(t), a version of the better-known Jagdpanzer 38(t) Hetzer assault gun. This one from Flammpanzer Kompanie 353 (353rd Flamethrowing Panzer Company) was captured while supporting the attacks of the 17th SS Panzer Grenadier Division near Gros Rederching against the American 44th Division.

A GI looks over the flame gun on the captured Flammpanzer 38(t). These were used in a number of engagements with American troops, including attacks on U.S.-occupied stretches of the Maginot Line.

On 13 January 1945, troops of the 44th Division inspect another Flammpanzer 38(t), captured in Gros Rederching.

The main German blow in Alsace was directed against the U.S. Seventh Army, but fighting also continued in the neighboring Saar region by elements of Patton's Third Army that were left behind. This is an M4A3 named *Ask Mae* of the 778th Tank Battalion, which was supporting the 95th Division in the fighting for the Saarlautern bridgehead on 2 January.

This Jagdpanzer 38(t) was knocked out near Kilstett during the fighting in the northeast suburbs of Strasbourg in January; it is probably from Panzer Jäger Bataillon 1553 (1553rd Tank Destroyer Battalion), attached to the 553rd Volksgrenadier Division, which attacked the town on 5 January as part of Operation Nordwind. A large chunk of armor has been blown off the front corner, testament to the thin armor plate on the hull side.

A group of M4A1 tanks of the 753rd Tank Battalion attached to the 36th Division in the town square of Lauterbourg in early January prior to the withdrawal caused by the German attack during Nordwind.

An M5A1 of the 749th Tank Battalion drives past an entrenched GI of the 44th Division with a .30-caliber Browning machine gun during the fighting in Alsace in January. The M5A1 is from the initial production batch fitted with the rare early turret, which had an armored cover on the turret side where an opening port had been located on the earlier M3A3 turret.

An overhead view of an M18 76mm gun motor carriage of the 827th Tank Destroyer Battalion (Colored), one of a number of segregated African-American units in the U.S. Seventh Army. This battalion fought in the battles of Hatten-Rittershoffen in January.

A detailed rear view of the M18 seen above. This particular battalion had been equipped with the towed 3-inch antitank gun but was re-equipped with the M18 prior to being deployed in France in Novemebr 1944.

An M5A1 light tank passes a truckload of German prisoners during the fighting near Strasbourg in January.

Tanks of Company A, 23rd Tank Battalion, 12th Armored Division, provide indirect fire support during operations near Gambsheim in early January.

The main Nordwind attack by the 17th SS Panzer Grenadier Division in the Saare Valley went badly from the start. On 5 January, a few of the monstrous Jagdtigers from schwere Panzer Jäger Abteilung 653 (653rd Heavy Tank Destroyer Battalion), accompanied by a captured M4 medium tank, supported the attack near Rimling. An M36 90mm gun motor carriage from the 776th Tank Destroyer Battalion carefully moved into a flanking position and, at a range of 900 yards, put a single armor-piercing round into the side of Jagdtiger number 134, causing an internal ammunition fire that destroyed the vehicle in a catastrophic explosion, blowing off the superstructure sides.

During the opening phase of the Hatten-Rittershoffen battle, the 714th Tank Battalion is seen moving up from Bischwiller toward Drusenheim on 8 January.

An M4A3 (76mm) medium tank of Company B, 781st Tank Battalion, advances past a column of destroyed American vehicles on 7 January while supporting the 274th Infantry during its clean-up operations inside Wingen-sur-Moder, which had been abandoned by SS Gebirgs Regiment 12 (12th SS Mountain Regiment) the night before.

An M4A3 of the 781st Tank Battalion passes through Wingen-sur-Moder following the German retreat on 7 January. This town marked the deepest penetration of the initial German attacks during Operation Nordwind.

An M31 tank-recovery vehicle of the 781st Tank Battalion helps clean up in Wingen-sur-Moder following the fighting there in early January.

An M5A1 light tank of the French First Army in Alsace in January.

This is an M7 105mm howitzer motor carriage of the 62nd RAA, French 1st Armored Division, French First Army, during a fire mission in Alsace with an enormous stack of expended fiberboard ammunition tubes nearby.

A German air raid set off ordnance near this M5A1 light tank in Betschdorf on 10 January, causing extensive damage.

Crew members of an M5A1 of Company D, 47th Tank Battalion, 14th Armored Division, whitewash their tank using mops during the fighting in Alsace in mid-January. The tank has already been reinforced with sandbag armor, a common practice of the Seventh Army in Alsace.

Two GIs from the 14th Armored Division inspect the wreckage in Hatten after the town was recaptured in March. In the background is an M4A3 medium tank of the 14th Armored Division while in the foreground is an M18 76mm gun motor carriage of the 827th Tank Destroyer Battalion (Colored).

A knocked-out Pz.Kpfw. IV in the ruins of Hatten following the fighting.

A scene in Hatten after the fighting had ended in late January. There are scattered bits of Sherman tanks of the 14th Armored Division in this field. In all likelihood, these were blown up using explosive charges by the Germans prior to retreating in order to prevent their recovery by the U.S. Army, a common practice on both sides.

Another view of the fields between Hatten and Rittershoffen where some of the most intense fighting of the Alsace campaign took place in the second and third weeks of January.

A Pz.Kpfw. IV knocked out during the fighting with the 14th Armored Division in Alsace in January.

Another example of a Pz.Kpfw. IV knocked out during the fighting with the 14th Armored Division in Hatten-Rittershofen in January.

A destroyed M4A3 medium tank of the 14th Armored Division in the ruins of Rittershoffen after the fighting. The level of violence within the towns is evident from the sheer number of hits on this tank, with at least five hits visible from the rear alone.

An M4A3 (76mm) of the 12th Armored Division knocked out during the brutal fighting in Herrlisheim in January.

A pair of M4A3's of the 12th Armored Division following the fighting in Herrlisheim. Most of the 43rd Tank Battalion was knocked out in this battle.

A column of tanks from the 12th Armored Division moves toward the Gambsheim bridgehead in January. The battle for Herrlisheim was the first significant combat for this inexperienced division.

The southern end of Herrlisheim was a ruin of burned-out 12th Armored Division tanks and wrecked buildings, evident in this photograph taken after the fighting.

Crews from 12th Armored Division recover a damaged M4A3 medium tank from the 43rd Tank Battalion. It had been knocked out two weeks earlier in the ferocious fighting around Herrlisheim that had destroyed the battalion on 17–18 January.

The survivors of the 43rd Tank Battalion, 12th Armored Division, in Oberschaffolsheim on 26 January. The battalion lost nearly forty tanks in the fighting for Herrlisheim.

A crewman of an M4A3 loads ammunition into his tank near Hatten on 20 January. This vehicle is from the 48th Tank Battalion, 14th Armored Division, and is marked with unusually prominent stars for this stage of the war.

An M15A1 combination gun motor carriage and an M16 machine-gun motor carriage of an antiaircraft artillery battalion supporting the 14th Armored Division move through Mertzwiller, France, on 20 January. These air-defense vehicles usually towed trailers with additional ammunition and supplies, as seen here.

A mid-production M10 3-inch gun motor carriage of Gen. Alexander Patch's Seventh Army uses some fencing to provide improvised camouflage during the fighting along the border between Alsace and Germany on 24 January.

An M10 3-inch gun motor carriage of the 636th Tank Destroyer Battalion conducts an overwatch of the fields outside Bischwiller on 28 January while supporting the 36th Infantry Division.

Gen. Walton "Bulldog" Walker's XX "Ghost" Corps encouraged the pattern-painting of armored equipment using whitewash, and this particular M2A1 half-track car was displayed as an example. The dark bands are from the original olive-drab finish.

Another view of the M2A1 seen above half-track, this time showing the left side.

Another view of the M2A1 from the previous page, pictured near Thionville on 12 January.

This Nashorn 88mm tank destroyer of schwere Panzerjäger Abteilung 654 (654th Heavy Tank Destroyer Battalion) was knocked out in a duel with a French M10 3-inch gun motor carriage tank destroyer of the 2e DB during the fighting near Riedwihr on 26 January in the Elsenheim woods during the final skirmishes in the Colmar pocket, one of six that that were knocked out that day after blocking the sector with their long-range guns.

Alsatian civilians returned to the ruins of the village of Mittelwihr on the eastern slopes of the High Vosges following the elimination of the Colmar pocket in February. The wrecked Pz.Kpfw. IV/70(A) was probably from Panzer Brigade 106, which fought in these final battles.

A column from Company C, 142nd Infantry, 36th Division, led by an M4A3 (76mm) tank moves through a snowy field near Dossenheim, France, between Saverne and Strasbourg on 29 January during the actions to recover ground lost during Nordwind. The tanks are probably from the 14th Armored Division, which was supporting the 36th Division in its attacks on the Gabsheim bridgehead.

A column of infantry from the 75th Division near Riedwihr is supported by M4A3 (76mm) tanks of the 709th Tank Battalion on 1 February.

One of the more curious vehicles captured by the 75th Division during the fighting near Ostheim on 31 January was this Hotchkiss H-39 light tank, known in German service as the Pz.Kpfw. 38H 735(f). These were most commonly seen in units fighting against partisans, but small numbers still remained in service at the beginning of 1945.

A snow-camouflaged M4A3 (76mm) tank of the 709th Tank Battalion is seen moving up to the front with troops of the 75th Division near Riedwihr during the operations in the Colmar pocket on 31 January.

Aside from the badly depleted Panzer Brigade 106, the only major panzer formation in the German Nineteenth Army during the Colmar fighting was schwere Panzerjäger Abteilung 654, which had forty-four Jagdpanthers and twenty-two Nashorn 88mm tank destroyers at the beginning of the fighting. The regiment was involved in heavy fighting through the last weeks of January, and by early February, it had no operational tank destroyers. This is one of the regiment's Jagdpanthers lost during the Colmar fighting.

A pair of French M10 3-inch gun motor carriages of the 11e Regiment de Chasseurs d'Afrique, 5e DB (11th African Chasseurs, 5th Armored Division), pass through the ruined village of Bettenhoffen on their way to Gambsheim on 1 February during the final clean-up battles along the Rhine.

German prisoners are escorted back by troops of the 75th Division near Bischwihr to the northeast of Colmar on 1 February. The M4A1 medium tanks are from the 709th Tank Battalion, which was supporting the 75th Division.

A well-camouflaged M4 (105mm) howitzer tank of the 48th Tank Battalion moves forward to positions near Hochdelden in Alsace-Lorraine as the U.S. Seventh Army prepares to resume its assault toward Germany. The lead tank has sandbag armor on the glacis plate, obscured by snow and a camouflage net.

An M3 half-track of the French 2nd Armored Division passes through a tank barrier in the outskirts of Colmar on 2 February. The rear tracks have a set of chains added for better traction in the snow.

An M5A1 of the French First Army in Colmar in Alsace during the fighting there in February at the conclusion of Nordwind. This particular tank has logs as a dubious source of added frontal protection.

GIs wait in a trench line with an M10 3-inch gun motor carriage tank destroyer in the background during the attacks on the Colmar pocket on 2 February.

A GI from the 12th Armored Division runs past a burned-out M4A3E2 assault tank of the 43rd Tank Battalion during the recapture of Herrlisheim in February.

A column of tanks of the 23rd Tank Battalion, 12th Armored Division, returns to Herrlisheim on 4 February as part of the effort to stamp out the remnants of the Gambsheim bridgehead. The German car in the foreground was a booby-trapped roadblock that detonated when struck by one of the passing tanks.

An M32 of the 25th Tank Battalion, 14th Armored Division, near Batzendorf on 9 February during the Alsace fighting.

A French M4A2 medium tank with accompanying infantry of the 5e DB moves toward the center of Colmar on 2 February during the fighting that led to the city's capture the following day.

This is one of a series of GI snapshots of the wreckage in the Colmar pocket after the fighting there on 10 February. This is a thoroughly destroyed M10 3-inch gun motor carriage tank destroyer.

This M4 medium tank suffered a catastrophic ammunition fire that blew off the turret during the Colmar fighting. In the background is a knocked-out M4A3 (76mm).

A destroyed M4A3 (76mm) in early February.

A 57mm antitank gun provides cover while an M4A3 medium tank advances forward.

The M5A1 command tank of Col. Charles Bromley, the commander of Combat Command B, 12th Armored Division, pauses for a map reading during the fighting against the Colmar pocket on 3 February.

After a two-week lull while the Colmar pocket was being cleared, the VI Corps stepped up its efforts to clean up unfinished business in early February by clearing the northern end of the Gambsheim bridgehead while the French 3e DIA cleared the south. Oberhoffen, held by the 10th SS Panzer Division (in the process of being relieved by the 257th Volksgrenadier Division), was the center of much of the fighting, which involved the 14th Armored and 36th Infantry Divisions on the American side. Here an M4A3 (76mm) burns in the foreground as medics evacuate casualties under the cover of an M10 3-inch gun motor carriage on 3 February during an action by the 142nd Infantry, 36th Division.

During the fighting in Alsace in the late winter and early spring of 1945, among the more dangerous antitank weapons encountered were the ex-Soviet 85mm antiaircraft guns that were deployed by hard-pressed Army Group G as improvised antitank weapons to screen the approaches to the Rhine. This one is being examined by troops of the 141st Infantry, 36th Division, on 20 February.

A GI from the 142nd Infantry passes by an M4A3 (76mm) tank knocked out in Oberhoffen when the 36th Division attacked the town on the night of 31 January–1 February. The town was bitterly defended by the 257th Volksgrenadier Division and the 10th SS Panzer Division.

An M4A3 of the 25th Tank Battalion, 14th Armored Division, passes through Oberhoffen in the wake of the fighting there in early February. It is already fit with the new sandbag armor.

A pair of M4A3 tanks from the 14th Armored Division support the 68th Armored Infantry Battalion during fighting in Oberhoffen on 6 February.

A radioman of the 68th Armored Infantry Battalion with an SCR-300 walkie-talkie radio directs an M4A3 tank of the 25th Tank Battalion, 14th Armored Division, during the fighting for Oberhoffen on 6 February.

The new panzer grenadier divisions were supposed to be allotted a company of fourteen assault guns for organic armored support. One of the more common types in Alsace was the Jagdpanzer 38(t), popularly called the Hetzer, which was a low-cost expedient in place of the older and more durable StuG III. This particular example in Oberhoffen on 13 February is being examined by a GI from Company F, 142nd Infantry, 36th Division, and was probably from Kampfgruppe Luttichau, which fought in the Gambsheim bridgehead.

A whitewashed M4A3 with dozer blade of the 714th Tank Battalion, Combat Command B, 12th Armored Division, passes through Colmar on 3 February after the city was liberated.

A whitewashed M5A1 light tank of the 714th Tank Battalion, 12th Armored Division, drives through Colmar on 3 February.

A pair of M16 machine-gun motor carriage antiaircraft half-tracks of the 12th Armored Division pass through Colmar on 3 February.

Armored infantrymen of the 46th Armored Infantry Battalion ride an M4A3 tank of the 714th Tank Battalion during the advance of Combat Command R, 12th Armored Division, in the Colmar-Mulhouse sector on 4 February.

In the wake of the liberation of Colmar, a delegation of dignitaries reviews the M4A2 tanks of the French 5th Armored Division. In the lead is Gen. Jean de Lattre de Tassigny, commander of the French First Army, and over his shoulder is the hero of Omaha Beach, Maj. Gen. Norman Cota, who at the time commanded the 28th Division.

A parade of M5A1 light tanks of the French 5th Armored Division celebrating the liberation of Colmar in early February.

An M3A1 half-track of the 119th Engineers, 12th Armored Division, rests in the town of Rouffech, France, on 5 February after the Colmar pocket had been sealed. The vehicle is fitted with a locally built stowage rack on the rear. This half-track is marked with the "bar and ball" geometric tactical insignia peculiar to the 12th Armored Division.

An M10 3-inch gun motor carriage of the 636th Tank Destroyer Battalion supporting the 143rd Infantry Regiment, 36th Division, moves through the rubble-strewn streets of Rohrwiller, France, on 4 February.

A snow-camouflaged M4A3 (76mm) of the 709th Tank Battalion supporting the 75th Division during the fighting in Alsace in February.

GIs of Company B, 68th Armored Infantry Battalion, accompany tanks of the 14th Armored Division during the recapture of Oberhoffen on 6 February, the scene of intense fighting a few weeks earlier.

This whitewashed M4A3 (76mm) with sandbag armor on the glacis plate was knocked out during February.

A rare view of an M4A3E2 Jumbo assault tank in action during the fighting in the Colmar area in February. The tank is covered with Sommerfield matting for attaching foliage camouflage.

A GI from the 75th Division inspects an abandoned Flakpanzer IV Wirbelwind in Hettenschlag on 9 February. The Wirbelwind ("Whirlwind") consisted of a quad 20mm FlaK 38 on a Pz.Kpfw. IV chassis.

French troops supported by an M10 3-inch gun motor carriage tank destroyer of the 11e Regiment de Chasseurs d'Afrique of the French 5th Armored Division during the fighting north of Strasbourg around Gambsheim on 9 February. The crew has added a captured German MG34 machine gun to its armament.

Another view of a pair of M10 tank destroyers of the 5e RCA on 9 February during the fighting to eliminate the last German bulge over the Rhine north of Strasbourg. Gambsheim was the scene of intense fighting several weeks earlier in which the 12th Armored Division took heavy losses.

A column of armor from the French 5th Armored Division, including M4A4 tanks and M10 tank destroyers, in the Gambsheim area on 9 February.

An elaborately camouflaged M4A3 of Company C, 25th Tank Battalion, 14th Armored Division, engages in gunnery practice in Huttendorf on 11 February during a lull in the fighting following the reduction of the Colmar pocket.

The M4A2 named *Les Eparges* (tactical number 43) of the 3rd Platoon, 3rd Company, 501st RCC, French 2nd Armored Division, near Münster on 15 February during operations near the Colmar pocket frontier.

In March, the U.S. Seventh Army continued its thrust northward through the Low Vosges into the Saar. Here troops of Combat Command A, 14th Armored Division, pause in Oberlauterach on 18 March.

Patch's Seventh Army was well equipped as it was the force nearest the key Mediterranean port of Marseilles. Here a new shipment of M4A3E8 tanks is dispatched from Marseilles to the front by rail on 10 February.

An M35 prime mover of the 575th Field Artillery Battalion, 35th Field Artillery Group, is seen here towing the tube from an M1 8-inch gun near Monnenheim, France, on 26 February. The M35 was an improvised prime mover consisting of an M10 tank destroyer with its turret removed and some modest features added, such as a new forward and rear towing pintle. They were used to tow heavy artillery until the definitive M6 high-speed tractor became available.

Another view of an M35 prime mover from the 575th Field Artillery Battalion in Monnenheim on 26 February from the rear provides a better view of the M1 8-inch gun. Because of the size of this weapon, the barrel and recoil assembly were towed separately from the carriage. Once in place, the barrel was moved onto the carriage using an M2 truck-mounted crane.

U.S. tank units were taking so many casualties to panzerfaust rocket launchers that various expedients were tested to defend against them. After having seen German tanks fitted with screened skirts, U.S. Army ordnance officers tested the idea of using screens for panzerfaust protection. But as shown here in a test against a captured Pz.Kpfw. IV near Sarrebourg on 2 January, the screens were completely ineffective in defending against shaped-charge warheads.

Following the reduction of the Colmar pocket, the Seventh Army stepped up its efforts to erase the German advances in the initial stages of Nordwind. The fortress city of Bitche was finally taken, and this heavily camouflaged Jagdpanzer 38(t) Hetzer assault gun was knocked out during the fighting there in early March by the XV Corps.

The heavy losses suffered by the 12th and 14th Armored Divisions to German antitank weapons during Nordwind fighting led to an extensive effort by the Seventh Army to develop expedient armor protection. The army's ordnance battalions developed a standardized kit consisting of metal frames welded to the turret and hull to contain sand bags. Some of the first tanks of the 14th Armored Division with the added sandbag armor in February also were camouflage-painted with bands of whitewash over the usual olive-drab finish like this M4A3E8 (76mm).

This M4A3 of the 25th Tank Battalion, 14th Armored Division, has a full array of sand bags while refitting at Huttendorf, France, on 11 February. The extra radio mast on the turret side suggests it is a forward observer tank.

Here an ordnance team welds the frame onto a new M4A3E8 of the 191st Tank Battalion in Graufthal, France, on 1 March.

With the frames in place, the ordnance crew loads sand bags into the frames of this 191st Tank Battalion M4A3E8.

This detail shot shows how the sand bags were stacked on the vehicle side.

Another view of a M4A3 (76mm) of the 14th Armored Division showing the configuration of the sand bags on the hull side. Some weeks later, the division began repainting its unit bumper codes on the gun barrels, a practice unique to this division.

The sand bags on the glacis plate were held on only by gravity, although some units filled them with concrete instead of sand for greater permanence.

An M4A3 (76mm) of the 14th Armored Division during exercises near Huttendorf, France, on 11 February. This tank has the side cage for sand bags, which have not been fitted so far. Because the sand bags covered the usual location of the divisional markings on the transmission cover, the 14th Armored Division moved these markings to the sides of the gun tube.

When the weather changed in March, many tanks were camouflage-painted in black over the usual olive drab. The engineer crews simply sprayed black paint straight over the sandbags and anything else in their way. Here, on 15 March in Montbronn, France, a crew from the 84th Engineer Camouflage Battalion sprays camouflage paint on an M5A1 of the 781st Tank Battalion that has been fitted with sandbag armor.

An M4A3E8 being camouflage-painted with black over olive drab on 15 March.

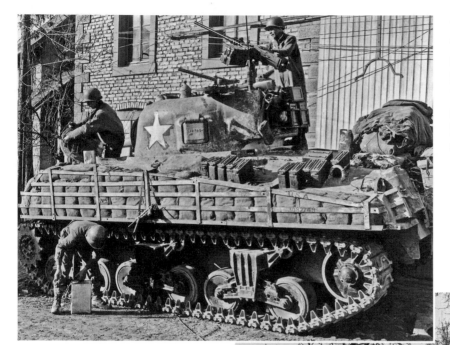

This M4A3 of the 25th Tank Battalion, 14th Armored Division, displays a full array of sandbag armor protection while the crew prepares the tank for action. This photo gives a clear view of the final style of vertical volute suspension, with the raised trailing roller arm and concave disc wheel covers.

The crew of this sandbagged M4A3E8 of Company B, 25th Tank Battalion, 14th Armored Division, conduct a radio check while bivouacked at Ohlungen on 14 March.

A new M4A3E8 tank is prepared by the 48th Tank Battalion, 14th Armored Division, before being committed to the fighting in the Saar. The crewman on the right is making certain that the new horizontal volute spring suspension is well lubricated.

Another upgrade undertaken in the wake of Nordwind was the provision of more flamethrowers on Seventh Army tanks to deal with the increasing number of German bunkers along the old Westwall. This old M4 of the 191st Tank Battalion is being fitted with an auxiliary E4-5 flamethrower that was mounted in the hull in place of the usual .30-caliber bow machine gun. The compressed air tanks were used to propel the fuel.

A new sandbagged M4A3 (76mm) of the 14th Armored Division in Niederbetsdorf in March.

A frontal view of the 191st Tank Battalion flame-tank with the flame-gun being tested. This old tank still has the original M34 narrow gun mantlet. This feature was not widely seen elsewhere in the theater because the neighboring 12th Army Group to the north had upgraded most of its Shermans under the "Quick Fix" program in 1943–44, which added a telescopic gun sight and the related wide M34A1 gun mantlet. Seventh Army veterans of Italy, like the 191st Tank Battalion, sometimes still had these old tanks.

The 191st Tank Battalion flame-tank tries out its new E4-5 flame gun on 13 February.

A 14th Armored Division M4A3 fitted with an E4-5 flamethrower gives a demonstration for commanding officers of the 44th and 100th Divisions against an old Maginot Line bunker near Hotton on 6 March. The Seventh Army was about to assault the German West-Stellung defense line, so additional flamethrowers were brought up to deal with bunkers.

A front view of the M7 with 9.75-inch mortar displayed to the senior commanders of the 6th Army Group and U.S. Seventh Army at Benny, France, on 28 February.

Another alternative for attacking German West-Stellung bunkers was this conversion of the M7 105mm howitzer motor carriage with a 9.75-inch heavy mortar. Developed by British Petroleum's Warfare Department, it fired a heavy incendiary projectile as seen on the side of the vehicle.

A close-up showing the heavy 9.75-inch mortar. In the event, it was not accepted for service.

Some ordnance officers were not entirely convinced of the value of sand bags to protect against panzerfaust antitank rockets. As a result, on 12 March, the 134th Ordnance Battalion, with the assistance of the 12th Armored Division's staff, took a knocked-out M4A3 tank that they fitted with spaced armor, sand bags, and other types of appliqué armor and subjected it to fire from various weapons. Here an M32 tank-recovery vehicle is used to put the target in place.

To simulate German antitank rockets, an American 2.36-inch bazooka was fired against the target tank.

To simulate German tank gun fire, this 12th Armored Division M4A3E8 fired a variety of projectile types at the target tank.

An ordnance officer inspects the damage on the target tank.

This close-up shows the spaced-steel armor that had been added to the hull front of the target tank.

The most serious shortcoming of the tank destroyers when used to provide infantry support in towns or close-grained terrain was the open roof. A number of attempts were made in the field to correct this problem. This is an armored roof devised by the 536th Ordnance HM Company of the Seventh Army fitted to M10 tank destroyers in February. This particular M10 is of the late-production type with the duckbill counterweights.

The M10 tank destroyers with the mid-production turrets had only the front portion of the armor kit added, as the roof opening was not sufficient to permit the full kit. This is an example from the 813th Tank Destroyer Battalion in Soultz, France, on 14 January.

Another view of the roof armor in use on an M10 3-inch gun motor carriage of the 813th Tank Destroyer Battalion in Soultz on 14 January.

A detailed front view of the improvised roof armor as fitted on an M10 3-inch gun motor carriage of the Seventh Army in February. Note also the extensive use of sandbag armor on this vehicle.

Another example of the use of improvised roof armor on an M10 3-inch gun motor carriage, in this case on a vehicle of the 12th Armored Division in Haguenau, France, while covering river crossings over the Moder River on 5 February in support of the 313th Infantry Regiment.

CHAPTER 3

Operation Grenade: Over the Roer

WITH THE DEFEAT of the German offensives in the Ardennes and Alsace at the end of January 1945, Eisenhower intended to conduct a three-phase operation to trap and destroy as much of the German army as possible on the western bank of the Rhine prior to major river-crossing operations in the early spring. The first phase of the plan was conducted by Field Marshal Bernard Montgomery's British/Canadian 21st Army Group, supported by Gen. William Simpson's U.S. Ninth Army. The mission was to close on the Rhine north of Düsseldorf in anticipation of Operation Plunder, the main British Rhine crossing scheduled for mid-March. The second phase was to close on the Rhine from Düsseldorf on south. This involved the 12th Army's Group's two remaining field armies, Gen. Courtney Hodges's U.S. First Army and Gen. George Patton's U.S. Third Army, with Gen. Alexander Patch's U.S. Seventh Army from the neighboring 6th Army Group supporting Patton. The third phase would be the advance into the plains of northern Germany and into central-southern Germany once the Rhine was breached.

The first phase of the Allied offensive began on 8 February with two operations aimed at reaching the western banks of the Rhine in the northern sector. Operation Veritable was Montgomery's effort to push his 21st Army Group through the forested Reichswald. Operation Grenade was a supporting effort by Simpson's Ninth Army to finally clear the Roer River—and especially the Roer River dams—as a prelude to future operations along the Rhine. Operation Veritable proved more difficult than anticipated because of the flooded terrain and stubborn German resistance, but the Ninth Army reached the Rhine on 2 March, followed by the Canadian First Army. The Ninth proposed to use nine of its twelve divisions to conduct a surprise crossing of the Rhine, but Eisenhower again deferred to the British plan to wait for Operation Plunder later that month. While Simpson's army was clearing the Roer, Patton's Third Army was making a push through the mountains and forests of Luxembourg as a follow-on to the Ardennes fighting, with its southern wing grinding its way through the formidable fortified regions of the Saar farther south.

American tank units were very unhappy with the performance of their Shermans in the Ardennes, finding them badly undergunned and underarmored compared to the rival Panther tank. With only the smallest number of new T26E3 Pershing tanks arriving, the units began taking their own approaches to the problem. As mentioned in the previous chapter, Patch's Seventh Army began a systematic effort to mount sand bags on their tanks to protect against the panzerfaust antitank rockets that were so common in urban fighting. Simpson's Ninth Army had a less systematic effort to use a combination of spare track links and sand bags to create improved protection. Some units also experimented with concrete. Ordnance officers in the Third Army convinced Patton that sand bags were not only ineffective, but a technical problem since the added weight led to premature suspension and transmission failures. As a result, the Third Army's tank units tended to rely on slabs of tank armor cut from derelict American and German tanks that had been knocked out in the Ardennes. The results were so encouraging that Patton's ordnance teams actually pilfered derelict panz-

ers from the neighboring Seventh Army's sector to strip them of armor plate.

The Wehrmacht had its own defensive program underway, focused mainly on fortification, not panzers. The West-Stellung program had been ongoing since the autumn of 1944 to reinforce the western German borders with field fortifications, antitank barriers, and a thick belt of antitank guns. This effort is often confused with the prewar Westwall fortifications, with both being erroneously dubbed the Siegfried Line. While the West-Stellung incorporated and rejuvenated the Westwall, it added considerably to its length and depth. The U.S. Army would lose far more tanks in encounters with the West-Stellung defense than against German panzers in February and March 1945 during the fighting in the foreground of the Rhine.

On 31 January, GIs of the 311th Infantry, 78th Division, walk past a pair of disabled Jagdpanzer 38(t)'s in the town of Kesternich following two days of savage fighting on the approaches to the vital Roer dams. The infantry was supported by tanks of the 736th Tank Battalion.

A StuG III assault gun with its roof blown off in Kinzweiler and photographed in early 1945. This vehicle was probably knocked out the previous November when the town was first taken.

Winter had still not relaxed its grip in early February, as seen in the case of this snow-swept M16 machine-gun motor carriage on the German frontier on 9 February.

An M4A3 of the 784th Tank Battalion (Colored) provides fire support for the 104th Division during fighting along the Rhine on 1 February. This was one of two black tank battalions in the northwest Europe campaign in 1944–45.

An M4A3 (76mm) of the 784th Tank Battalion (Colored) along the Rhine in early 1945. This tank is fitted with metal chevron track and duckbill extenders.

An M4A3 with M1 dozer of the African-American 784th Tank Battalion (Colored) is seen trying to extract a two-and-a-half-ton truck bogged down in the mud in Merode, Germany, on 1 February.

An M18 76mm gun motor carriage of the 704th Tank Destroyer Battalion passes by a derelict Pz.Kpfw. IV in Nennig on 2 February. The M18 has been irregularly painted with whitewash for winter camouflage.

Another view of the same M18, this time from the other side, shows the irregular whitewash camouflage. This was actually based on the official winter camouflage scheme ordered by the 12th Army Group, which suggested leaving bands of olive drab to break up the overall whitewash finish.

Another M18 of the 704th Tank Destroyer Battalion outside Nennig on 2 February. The GI in the foreground is preparing a stack of M1 antitank mines.

An M8 75mm howitzer motor carriage of Troop E, 106th Cavalry Reconnaissance Group, carries out a fire mission from the woods near Karlsbrunn, Germany, on 2 February. The tubes in the foreground are fiberboard 75mm ammunition containers.

A Panther knocked out in the winter of 1944–45 along the German frontier.

A pair of Panther Ausf. G knocked out in he fighting along the German frontier in the winter of 1945.

During the clean-up operations in the Ardennes, American troops found this abandoned M8 armored car that had been captured by the Germans and put into use.

This whitewashed M16 machine-gun motor carriage of the 457th Anti-Aircraft Artillery Automatic Weapons Battalion has a quiet time overlooking the fields around Canach, Luxembourg, on 3 February following the Battle of the Bulge.

Riflemen of the 9th Infantry, 2nd Division, in snowsuits board an M4A1 (76mm) of the 741st Tank Battalion during operations near Schonesseiffen on 2 February.

Following the heavy fighting in Belgium, the crew of an M4 (105mm) assault gun of HQ Company, 69th Tank Battalion, 6th Armored Division, repairs the transmission of their tank (tactical number 58) near Bastogne on 4 February.

Ordnance units of the Ninth Army developed an armor appliqué consisting of steel track welded to the armor covered with sandbags and a final cover of camouflage net, as seen on these M4A3 (76mm)'s of the 747th Tank Battalion near Schleiden, Germany, on 31 January. This appliqué was also commonly seen on tanks of the 2nd Armored Division in early 1945.

Ordnance officers of Patton's Third Army discouraged the use of sandbag armor, but the outcry after the heavy tank losses in the Battle of the Bulge led to the development of other expedients. In February, the ordnance units began stripping knocked-out American and German tanks of armor plate and welding it to the glacis plate and turret front of about 110 tanks, with priority given to M4A3E8 (76mm)'s and M4A3 (76mm)'s. The three armored divisions with Patton's Third Army, the 4th, 6th, and 11th, each received 36 of these. This particular example served with 11th.

This other view of an 11th Armored Division M4A3E8 (76mm) shows the appliqué steel armor added to the Third Army's tanks. All tanks received the hull armor, but only some received the turret armor. The glacis armor was often from the glacis plate of a knocked-out M4, complete with the associated headlight guards and other features.

An M4A3E8 of the 11th Armored Division with additional steel armor welded to the glacis plate and differential housing on the front of the tank in March.

This close-up of the 11th Armored Division M4A3E8 shows how the added armor was attached to completely cover the cast differential housing of the tank for better protection.

This is an example of a knocked-out M4 105mm assault tank that has been cannibalized for armor for the Third Army's up-armoring effort. In March, the Third Army acquired another batch of derelict M4 tanks from the Seventh Army and did a second round of up-armoring.

Another example of an M4 cannibalized for armor for the Third Army's program. After running out of knocked-out tanks in their own sector, Third Army ordnance units began scavenging tanks in the neighboring Seventh Army's sector since the units there preferred to use sand bags.

Patton's Third Army decided to rearm their 75mm M4 tanks with the 76mm gun, and a single M4A3 pilot was completed by ordnance in February. The conversion required the addition of a large slab of steel on the rear of the turret to act as a counterweight. Although feasible, the arrival of large numbers of M4A3 (76mm)'s made the conversions unnecessary, and the program was halted before more conversions were done. The accumulated 76mm guns were used to rearm about a hundred M4A3E2 assault tanks.

The Third Army's ordnance conversion for the 76mm gun on the smaller 75mm turret included the addition of a large slab of steel to the rear bustle to balance the turret by compensating for the added frontal weight of the long 76mm gun tube.

This is an M4A3E8 of the 4th Armored Division with a typical Third Army package of armor on the hull and turret.

This is a good example of an M4A3 (76mm) with the Third Army's up-armor package stationed with the 303rd Military Police Company at Patton's headquarters in Luxembourg City. The glacis plate came straight off another M4, complete with the various attachments and fittings.

An interesting example of a 3rd Armored Division M4 tank with a substantial slab of appliqué armor added to the hull front.

An example of the added appliqué after combat use. Several gouges from large-caliber hits can be seen. Of the various expedient types, this approach was by far the most effective enhancement to Sherman protection.

Another alternative to steel plate and sand bags was to cover the glacis plate with a layer of concrete stiffened with steel reinforcing bar, as seen on this example from the 11th Armored Division.

This provides some detail of the thickness of the added layer of steel-reinforced concrete.

This close-up shows the concrete armor that was layered on the glacis plate and hull side of an M4A3E8 of the 11th Armored Division in March.

A rear view of the same 11th Armored Division M4A3E8 with the concrete armor. The application was so well done that it is hard to see, but it can be recognized since it covers the narrow stub fender usually evident protuding from the hull side on the M4A3E8 with its wider track.

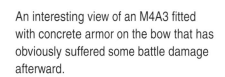

An interesting view of an M4A3 fitted with concrete armor on the bow that has obviously suffered some battle damage afterward.

Concrete was not a guarantee of protection against a panzerfaust, as seen in this example of a hull penetration on the side of an M4A3E8 that had a layer of concrete and steel rebar on the right hull side. A small panzerfaust penetration can be seen.

The upgrades on the Sherman after the Battle of the Bulge included a reconfiguration of the turret machine guns because of the inconvenient location of the external .50-caliber heavy machine gun pintle mount. The factory fit had the pintle on the rear of the turret roof, obliging the crew to exit the vehicle to fire it if the target was forward of the tank. This shows the recommended solution, moving the .50-caliber pintle mount in front of the loader's hatch. An additional .30-caliber was recommended for the tank commander, and a .50-caliber aircraft machine gun was substituted for the usual .30-caliber coaxial machine gun.

The uparmoring procedure of Patton's Third Army was so well regarded by Bradley's 12th Army Group headquarters that it was recommended as a standard package for tanks before being sent into combat. This particular vehicle was used as the model for these conversions with a report sent back to Washington.

Units outside Patton's Third Army tended to rely on other forms of appliqué armor, especially sand bags. This M4A3E8 is a tank of Company A, 18th Tank Battalion, 8th Armored Division, at Bocholtz, Netherlands, on 23 February.

A scene all too common in the final months of the war in Germany: a knocked-out M4A3 (76mm) of the 7th Armored Division. Many tanks were lost in skirmishes with small groups of German defenders armed with panzerfaust antitank rockets. About 11 percent of American tank casualties in 1945 were due to panzerfausts and other close-range antitank weapons.

The first unit scheduled to receive the M24 was the 744th Tank Battalion, one of only two battalions still equipped solely with light tanks. It re-equipped with the M24 light tank in January and first deployed it in combat in late February during Operation Grenade, the assault over the Roer River. Here a crew test-fires the gun during training near Eschwiller, Germany, on 12 February.

The tanks of the 69th Tank Battalion, 6th Armored Division, remain idle in a rail yard in Draufflet, Luxembourg. Their crews had been pressed into service as infantry in the fighting across the nearby German frontier. The tanks are a typical mixture of types thanks to the many replacements received during the Ardennes campaign. To the left is a whitewashed M4A3E8 with appliqué turret armor, the newest version of the Sherman to see service in the Ardennes.

A pair of Panther Ausf. G tanks from the 2nd Panzer Division knocked out in the fighting around Marnach on the German-Luxembourg frontier during the battles for the Our River with the 6th Armored Division on 6 February. The fighting for the Vianden bulge was the final phase of the Ardennes counteroffensive, aimed at pushing through the Siegfried Line into Germany near Bitburg.

A Panzer IV/70 (V) tank destroyer blown open by an internal ammunition fire lies in a crater near Marnach during the fighting with the 6th Armored Division in early February.

Another Panzer IV/70 (V) is seen here in Marnach, a casualty of the fighting along the Our River in early February. An internal ammunition fire has blown the superstructure off the hull. Behind it is an abandoned 75mm PaK 40 antitank gun.

One of the less common versions of the Hanomog armored half-tracks was the Sd.Kfz. 251/21, armed with a triple Drilling MG151S. This one, abandoned near Kalborn during the fighting along the German-Luxembourg frontier in early February is missing the usual armored shield around the gun mount.

An M4 (right) and M4A3 (76mm) (left) of the 68th Tank Battalion, 6th Armored Division, in the ruins of Heinerscheid, Luxembourg, during the fighting by Patton's Third Army along the Our River on 10 February.

A pair of M4 (105mm) howitzer tanks provide fire support from water-logged fields on the German border in February. The ground nearby is littered with spent shell casings and packing tubes. The crew of *Houston-Kid II* has improvised a bridge over the water using a timber.

On 16 February, troops of the 80th Division look over a self-propelled 37mm FlaK 43 Möbelwagen ("furniture truck") abandoned in Hosingen, Luxembourg. This vehicle was based on the Pz.Kpfw. IV tank but with a modified superstructure.

A Bergepanzer III knocked out in the outskirts of Hosingen in mid-February by an American air strike. This is the turretless tank-recovery version of the Pz.Kpfw. III tank.

An interior view showing the work platform in the captured Bergepanzer III.

A Jagdpanzer 38(t) Hetzer blown apart near Hosingen, Luxembourg, possibly a victim of air strikes along this road in mid-February.

An officer examines an abandoned Panther Ausf. G tank in the outskirts of Hosingen following the fighting for the Vianden bulge. This tank may have been from the 2nd Panzer Division or Führer Grenadier Brigade.

An M10 3-inch gun motor carriage of Patton's Third Army fires on German positions during the fighting along the Sauer River near Echtermach, Luxembourg, on 7 February.

This M4A3 of the 41st Tank Battalion, 11th Armored Division, had slipped off the muddy road near Trois Vierges on 7 February and is seen here in the process of being hoisted out of the ditch and recovered.

A view of the recovery scene after the tank has been extracted from the ditch.

A platoon of M4 medium tanks provides indirect fire support from positions in Luxembourg over the German border on 19 February.

As weather improved, the winter whitewash was gradually removed from vehicles, in this case from an M2A1 half-track car of the 489th Anti-Aircraft Artillery Battalion, attached to the 4th Armored Division on 8 February. This shows the battalion's cartoon unit insignia.

An M12 155mm gun motor carriage nicknamed *Choo-Choo-Bam* provides fire support for Patton's Third Army during fighting in Echternath, Luxembourg, on 8 February. This vehicle has been fitted with extended end connectors for better operation in mud.

After a false start in December 1944, ordnance teams began a more systematic attempt to distribute the new sixty-round T34 Calliope rocket launcher to various tank units in the European theater. This particular example is mounted on a tank of the 702nd Tank Battalion supporting the 80th Division in Patton's Third Army in February. In general, the launchers were unpopular with tank commanders, who felt that the artillery mission should be performed by artillery units and not tank units.

A close-up of the turret front of one of the 702nd Tank Battalion's Calliopes. An arm connected the launcher assembly to the gun barrel for elevation and depression.

A close-up of one of the 4.5-inch rockets fired by the T34 Calliope launcher.

The later batches of Calliope launch kits, which included a flame deflector mounted on the engine deck to prevent rocket exhaust from entering the engine compartment. It also doubled as a platform for loading.

Another view of a T34 Calliope being loaded. The flame deflector frame is very evident in this view.

The crew loads rockets into the T34 Calliope tubes.

A T34 Calliope mounted on an M4 of the 702nd Tank Battalion in February. This tank has sandbag armor on the glacis plate as well as wire mesh for attaching camouflage.

A pair of M4 tanks with the T34 launcher move into firing position while supporting the 80th Division on 19 February. The fighting in the Eifel was the first time that the Calliopes were used in this sector, supporting the 5th and 80th Divisions.

A dramatic nighttime view of a T34 Calliope being fired.

A platoon of M4 tanks of the 702nd Tank Battalion moves into position to fire against targets along the German Westwall fortifications near Wallendorf on 19 February when Patton's Third Army was pushing out of the Vianden area of Luxembourg.

One of the T34 Calliope launchers begins to fire its rockets. The rockets were usually salvoed in half-second intervals.

A platoon of tanks from the 702nd Tank Battalion fitted with T34 Calliope launchers passes through Korperich, Germany, on 21 February near the German-Luxembourg border in the Eifel region.

This Calliope of the 14th Armored Division is being reloaded near Dettwiller on 16 February.

With the port of Antwerp finally open, supplies of new equipment began flooding into Europe. Here a brand-new M4A3E8 is unloaded at the Antwerp docks on 9 February.

An M12 155mm gun motor carriage slogs through the glutinous mud in Luxembourg on 9 February while supporting the 5th Infantry Division in its attacks on pillboxes along the Siegfried Line. The M12 was very popular in the battles along the German frontier for attacking pillboxes and other reinforced positions of the Siegfried Line.

A unit of M4A3 tanks of the 10th Armored Division near Saarburg on 14 February during the fighting for the Saar-Moselle triangle by Patton's Third Army.

Much to the relief of some tank crews, the first shipment of twenty new T26E3 tanks arrived at the port of Antwerp in early February with the Zebra mission. This is one of the Pershing tanks being loaded onto an M25 tank transporter in Antwerp harbor on 9 February, using one of the less-often-seen M26A1 unarmored tractors.

A pair of M25 tank transporters with T26E3 tanks loaded aboard brings them to the 3rd and 9th Armored Divisions for conversion training on the new tank at the end of February.

One of the new T26E3 tanks is taken for a test drive. When type-classified later in 1945, the T26E3 became the M26 Pershing.

A view inside the M26 Pershing from the commander's station in the rear right side looking forward toward the gunner's station.

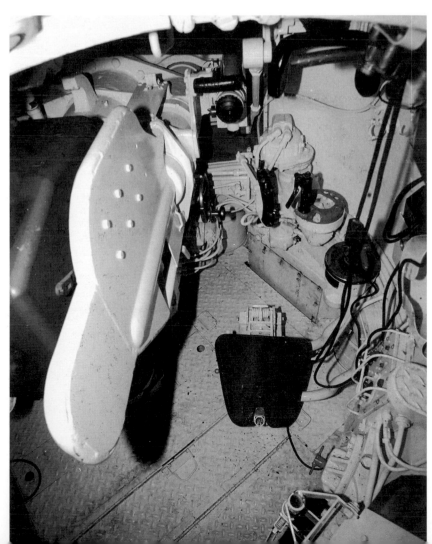

This M29C amphibious Weasel is attached to the 102nd Division as an ambulance during the fighting along the Roer River on 15 February.

The 56th Signals Battalion has modified its M29 Weasels with a frame on the rear to unspool standard communication wire reels, as seen here on the German frontier on 17 February.

Here an M2A1 half-track of the 10th Armored Division crosses a pontoon bridge over the Saar River near Taben during the advance by Patton's Third Army.

The crew of a snow-covered M18 of the 638th Tank Destroyer Battalion, attached to the 5th Armored Division, enjoys some hot chow during a lull on 15 February during the attacks toward the Roer River. The division finally crossed the river on 27 February in the wake of Operation Grenade.

An M16 antiaircraft half-track stands guard duty with the 390th Anti-Aircraft Artillery Battalion in Saarlautern on 15 February. Patton's Third Army was bottled up on the approaches to the Siegfried Line here, finally cracking though in March. The unit insignia, a cartoon dragon on tracks wielding machine guns, can be seen on the hull side.

An M20 armored utility car named *Rusty* of the headquarters of the 6th Cavalry Group, serving with Patton's Third Army in Germany on 17 February. The unit has widened the ring mount so that it traverses the whole parapet, at the front of which they have also added a plastic windshield.

Some units customized their half-tracks for special roles, such as this command post vehicle of the 85th Reconnaissance Squadron, 5th Armored Division, at Hoensbroek, Holland, on 19 February. The basic M3 half-track has had an extended section added to the rear to permit the officers to stand while viewing maps.

Infantry clamber aboard an M4A3 (76mm) of the 2nd Armored Division during Operation Grenade near Aachen on 20 February.

The U.S. Army requested fifty British Sherman Crocodile flamethrower tanks for the D-Day landings. These used the same flame gun and fuel trailer as the more familiar Churchill Crocodile, only fitted to a Sherman tank. The project was delayed, and this is one of the prototypes during trials.

The U.S. Army's Crocodile program was cancelled after D-Day, but four tanks that had already been converted were handed over to the U.S. Army in the autumn of 1944.

This shows the flame gun of the Sherman Crocodile, which was mounted in a small traversible fitting to the right of the bow gunner's station on the right corner of the hull front. These four tanks were issued to the 739th Tank Battalion (SMX) for operations along the Siegfried Line in February.

One of the few times that the American Crocodiles were used in combat was during Operation Grenade in February when the 739th Tank Battalion conducted the attack on the citadel in Julich, Germany. Two of the flame tanks are seen here on 24 Feburary.

An M29 of the 30th Division unloads from the rear of an LVT-4 near Pier, Germany, during the Roer River operations on 23 February.

A small number of Crab flail tanks were obtained from British sources and served with 739th Tank Battalion (Special). An attempt to use them to breach a minefield on 30 January failed when two Crabs were knocked out by German guns, two were lost to mines, and one suffered a mechanical breakdown. The remaining Crabs were used in February and March in attempts to clear minefields on the approaches to the Roer and Rhine Rivers. This is a Crab in operation near Vicht on the Roer River approaches on 21 February.

A number of units created improvised bridgelayers by fitting M31 and M32 tank-recovery vehicles with simple fittings to attach treadway bridge sections. This is an example based on an M31 with the 17th Armored Engineer Battalion. These were primarily used to breach German antitank ditches, which were a common obstacle along the German frontier in 1944–45.

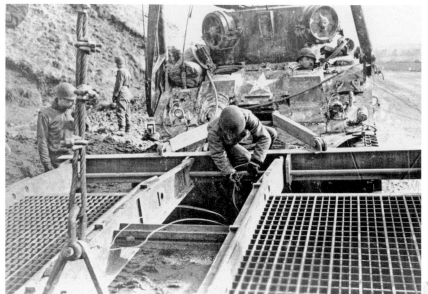

Here the crew of an M32 tank-recovery vehicle of the 22nd Engineer Battalion, 5th Armored Division, attaches a section of M2 treadway bridge to the hinge assembly at the front of the vehicle during operations near Hoensbruck, Netherlands, on 21 February. These improvised bridgelaying tanks were used to breach antitank ditches during Operation Grenade.

A close-up of the hinge assembly at the front of the M32 used to mount the treadway bridge to the vehicle.

The new M4A3E8 tanks began being issued in significant numbers in January 1945. These used the new horizontal volute spring suspension, which improved the mobility of the M4A3 in muddy terrain due to the use of a wider track. These two tankers from the 66th Armored Regiment, 2nd Armored Division, are taking part in a press briefing at Teuven, Netherlands, on 22 February, where they are showing the difference in size between the 75mm and 76mm projectiles while standing in front of one of the new M4A3E8 tanks.

The maintenance company of the 749th Tank Battalion is parked in the shattered town of Kerbach on 22 February while supporting the 70th Division. To the left is an M32B1 tank-recovery vehicle; to the right is an M3 half-track.

A pair of StuG III assault guns knocked out by American artillery during the fighting around Wallendorf on 21 February.

Facing an increasing number of river obstacles, the U.S. Army began deploying more LVT's (landing vehicle, tracked) for river-crossing operations. These are a platoon of LVT-2 amtracs being unloaded near the Roer on 23 February while supporting the 30th Division.

Another column of amtracs, this time the LVT-4 version, near the Roer on 23 February.

The area attacked during Operation Grenade had been heavily fortified in the autumn of 1944 and the early winter of 1944–45 as part of the Düren Fortification Sector of the new West-Stellung defensive lines. Among the new defenses were a number of Panzerturm defenses consisting of obsolete tank turrets mounted on concrete bunkers. This is a Festung-Panzer-Drehturm 4803 (Rotating Tower Panzer Fortress 4803) captured by the 30th Division on 26 February near Niederzier, part of the Roer defenses north of Düren. Obsolete Pz.Kpfw. I turrets were recycled for use in fortifications by adding a thicker front armor plate.

An overhead view of the Festung-Panzer-Drehturm 4803 showing the interior of the turret and the changes to the side, including the addition of armored covers over the old openings. A total of 143 of these were deployed in the West-Stellung, mainly in the Düren Fortification Sector along the Roer River.

Old Pz.Kpfw. II light tank turrets were rearmed with surplus 37mm guns and deployed as the Festung-Panzer-Drehturm 4804. This example is mounted on a Regelbau 283 bunker at the Hillersleben proving ground. This is a rear view of the bunker showing the lower access door; in combat, the front of the concrete bunker would be completely enclosed in earth.

Besides using surplus tank turrets, a number of specially designed turrets patterned on the Panther turret were also used on the West-Stellung. This Pantherturm I on an OT-Stahlunterstand Typ D was being emplaced by Festung Pionier Kommandateur XIX, five kilometers west of Bonn along Highway 56 but was captured by the U.S. Army before it was finished in 1945. This example uses the Ostwallturm, which was based on the Panther tank turret but with thicker roof armor and other changes.

The OT-Stahlunterstand Typ D was a two-story pillbox with this second steel box containing the crew quarters positioned under the turret and fighting compartment box. The two steel boxes would be completely buried, leaving only the turret exposed.

The Düren Fortification Sector had an extensive array of fixed antitank gun positions emplaced as part of the West-Stellung defensive effort. Many of these were surplus tank guns emplaced on improvised pedestal mounts. This SK-L IIa pedestal 88mm KwK 43/3 gun from the Jagdpanther tank destroyer is mounted on a standard Betonfundament concrete pad. This gun was part of the Roer defenses, deployed in a field near Erkelenz, and was knocked out during the fighting on 26 February during the U.S. Ninth Army's Operation Grenade. The wooden framing was part of a frame for camouflage netting erected over the gun before it was prepared for action.

A typical example of an 88mm pedestal gun of the Fest.PaK Verband XIV in the Roer River sector that was overrun in the 1945 fighting. The wood frame from the camouflage tent lies on the ground near the pit.

One of the fundamental problems of the pedestal-mounted antitank guns was their vulnerability because of lack of concrete or armored protection. As a result, camouflage was usually the only recourse, as seen on this SK-L IIa 88mm KwK 43/3 mounted on a concrete pad. This gun was derived from the Jagdpanther and is still fitted with its distinctive armored mantlct.

Another example of an SK-L IIa pedestal 88mm KwK 43/3 gun from the Jagdpanther tank destroyer knocked out in the Roer fighting.

About 400 of these Sockellafette Ia armed with the 50mm KwK 39/1 Bordkanone were ordered for border defense, and about 150 were assigned to the West-Stellung in 1945. The gun is a surplus aircraft gun of the type used to arm the Me 410 heavy fighter, but armed with the usual 50mm antitank ammunition.

The West-Stellung fortification effort incldued an extensive array of antitank ditches and obstacles. These could be quite effective, as seen here with this disabled M4A3 in an antitank barrier near Sinz, Germany, on 9 February during the operations by Patton's Third Army in this sector.

A key capability in offensive armored operations is rapidly erecting bridges over rivers. The U.S. Army relied heavily on treadway bridges like the one seen here over the Roer River during Operation Grenade on 24 February. Grenade finally succeeded in overwhelming the German defense along the Roer after months of bloody fighting by the Ninth Army. The M4 of the 750th Tank Battalion is seen fitted with a dozer blade, another innovation first introduced in the summer of 1944 to provide tank battalions with the ability to rapidly clear road obstructions and tank obstacles during offensive operations.

An M4A1 of the 771st Tank Battalion engages targets in the town of Baal during the fighting on the eastern bank of the Roer River on 24 February during Grenade. The attack beyond Linnich was able to exploit a gap between the XII SS Korps and the LXXXI Korps on the road to Muenchen-Gladbach.

An M4A3 (76mm) of Company C, 771st Tank Battalion, sets out from Linnich while supporting the 84th Division during the Roer offensive.

An M4A3 (76mm) crosses a treadway bridge at Linnich on 24 February during Grenade.

An M4A3 (76mm), probably from the 771st Tank Battalion, leads a column through Linnich on 24 February, the day after the town had been seized by the 84th Division at the start of Grenade. The first vehicular bridge was put across the Roer hours before, and tanks and tank destroyers were rushed into the town in anticipation of a German counterattack since both the 9th and 11th Panzer Divisions were stationed to the west of Cologne.

An M4A1 (76mm) moves past one of the double Bailey bridges erected over the Roer near Jülich. The tank is fitted with sand bags on the glacis and carries several unditching beams on the nose.

An M4 named *Lil-Patty-Lou* of the 2nd Armored Division is directed by an MP to the treadway bridge over the Roer at Jülich on 26 February.

Two M4's from Combat Command B, 2nd Armored Division, cross a treadway bridge into the battered town of Jülich on 26 February following several days of fighting. It was one of the key crossing points on the Roer River and was nearly leveled.

An M4A3 (76mm) of the 701st Tank Battalion near Lövenich on 25 February. The battalion had lost twenty-two tanks the day before to German antitank guns and obstacles while supporting the 405th Infantry near Hottorf, a bloody reminder that the war was not yet over.

An M4 dozer tank of the 5th Armored Division moves forward through Ubach during Operation Grenade on 24 February.

A well-protected M10 3-inch gun motor carriage passes through Düren, Germany, while supporting the 8th Infantry Division's operations on 24 February. This vehicle is still fitted with the Culin hedgerow cutters and carries an extensive amount of sand bags and logs to offer further protection against German panzerfaust antitank rockets.

An M4 leads a column through the ruins of Düren, which was largely destroyed during the fighting in this sector.

An M10 3-inch gun motor carriage of the 801st Tank Destroyer Battalion moves down a street in Jülich on 24 February during the Roer offensive.

GIs from the 415th Infantry Regiment, 104th Division, walk past a pair of disabled M4A3 tanks in Arnoldsweiler on 25 February. Careful inspection of the glacis plate of the two tanks shows that they have been fitted with poured concrete armor as protection against panzerfausts.

An M2A1 half-track of Battery B, 276th Field Artillery Battalion, XII Corps, Third Army, loads up on 105mm ammunition to transport forward to the battery's firing positions near Baustert, Germany, on 24 February.

A StuG III knocked out near Rheindahlen in late February, with an M5A1 light tank behind it.

One of the new M4A3E8 tanks operating with the 8th Armored Division near Roermund on 26 February. Some of the tanks were not fitted with the muzzle brake so often associated with this type.

An M30 cargo carrier of the 557th Armored Field Artillery Battalion moves through the fog-shrouded town of Linnich on the morning of 26 February. This was one of the main crossing points over the Roer during Operation Grenade. In the foreground to the left is an M12 155mm gun motor carriage of the battalion.

An M30 cargo carrier of the 557th Armored Field Artillery Battalion moves over a treadway bridge outside Linnich on 26 February. This unit welded rods along the superstructure for crew stowage. This particular vehicle is fitted with extended end connectors for better mobility in the mud.

An M12 155mm gun motor carriage (*The Persuader*) of Battery B, 557th Armored Field Artillery Battalion, moves across a treadway bridge during the fighting near Linnich on 26 February. The crew has stowed some wood pallets over the entrenching spade, probably for use in crew quarters during the wet winter weather.

An M36 90mm gun motor carriage shepherds a column of half-tracks from the 23rd Armored Engineers of the 3rd Armored Division in the ruins of Düren on 26 February. In the foreground is an M3A1 half-track named *Achtung!* of the 23rd Engineers, 3rd Armored Division. The logs on the hull side were probably being carried for an engineer construction project rather than as stand-off armor. Düren had been hotly contested because of its strategic position on the Roer River. It was a staging area for the VII Corps' Roer crossing during Grenade in late February.

The final push for the Roer through the Hürtgenwald on 26 February. Weary GIs of the 39th Infantry, 9th Division, prepare to move forward near Rath on 27 February while being supported by a pair of M4A3E2 assault tanks of the 746th Tank Battalion. That day, the division finally captured one of the Roer dams at Schwammenauel—little solace for the heavy casualties the division had suffered in the bloody Hürtgen fighting.

This Tiger from the 4th Company of schwere Panzer Abteilung 506 (506th Heavy Panzer Battalion) knocked out a T26E3 Pershing named *Fireball* of the 3rd Armored Division on 26 February near Elsdorf, Germany, but while attempting to withdraw, it was immobilized and abandoned. *Fireball* was repaired and put back into action, but this Tiger fell into American hands. Another Tiger from the unit was knocked out the following day in an encounter with another Pershing.

A jeep column passes an abandoned German 75mm PaK 40 antitank gun following the capture of Saarburg on 22 February by Patton's Third Army.

An M5 high-speed tractor tows an M1 155mm howitzer over a treadway pontoon bridge across the Roer on 23 February. The 155mm howitzer was the standard heavy weapon of American divisions, each of which usually had three battalions of 105mm howitzers and one battalion of the 155mm howitzer. The M5 high-speed tractor was its standard prime mover in 1944–45.

An M16 machine-gun motor carriage of the 465th Anti-Aircraft Artillery Battalion waits while German POWs dig a protective revetment in Saarburg on 26 February.

A half-track column from Combat Command B, 10th Armored Division, on 26 February in Irsch, Germany, during the fight by Patton's Third Army for the Saar-Moselle Triangle.

M4A3 (76mm) tanks of the 771st Tank Battalion in a bivouac in Rurich on 26 February during Operation Grenade while supporting the 84th Division. The white stars on the tanks have been hastily overpainted to remove prominent targets for German antitank gunners. A 57mm antitank gun can be seen in the foreground.

An M4A3 of the 5th Armored Division moves through Lovenich on 27 February during the exploitation phase of Grenade. The crew has created a large rack on the back of the turret to stow personal gear.

The M6 high-speed tractor finally arrived in the European theater in 1945. Here one from the 266th Field Artillery Battalion is seen towing a 240mm howitzer through Düren during the advance on the Rhine on 27 February.

One of the more unusual German armored vehicles active in the fighting along the Roer was the Sturmtiger. This was built using worn-out Tiger tank hulls fitted with a new superstructure to accomodate the massive Raketenwerfer 61 mortar. The "Oberempt Monster" was deployed with Sturm-Mörser-Kompanie 1001 in the Düren sector in February.

Another view of the Sturmtiger captured in Oberempt near Düren in late February by the 30th Division. This unusual vehicle attracted a great deal of attention by photographers and technical intelligence teams.

A close-up of the barrel of the Raketenwerfer 61 mortar. Although designated as a mortar because of its inclination of fire, the weapon was actually a breech-loaded, rifled rocket launcher. It was derived from the Rheinmetall-Borsig R300 rocket-propelled depth-charge launcher developed for the German navy as a coastal defense antisubmarine weapon in the Atlantic Wall. The small holes around the lip of the barrel were vents to allow the rocket exhaust to escape.

The "Oberempt Monster" was knocked out on the morning of 26 February when the driver accidentally steered the huge vehicle into a drainage ditch along Neusserstrasse in Oberempt while trying to withdraw from the village. A Sherman from Company C, 743rd Tank Battalion, suddenly appeared behind it while supporting the attack by the 1st Battalion, 117th Infantry, 30th Division, and pumped several rounds into the engine compartment, as seen here. The crew managed to escape, except for one crewman who was shot when trying to throw a grenade at the pursuing Americans.

A frontal view of the captured Sturmtiger shows the massive size of the breach. It was evacuated by the 464th Ordnance Evacuation Company in March and sent back to Britain for technical evaluation. Parts of its unique gun system are still preserved in the United Kingdom.

This GI appears ready to do a carnival flying cannonball performance. This provides a good idea of the size of the mortar tube, which was 380 millimeters (15 inches) in diameter.

A side view of the abandoned Sturmtiger shows how the fixed superstructure was added to the hull in place of the usual Tiger tank turret.

A rear corner view of the abandoned Sturmtiger. This vehicle attracted considerable attention because of its rarity and the novelty of its weapon.

An unusual shot of the Sturmtiger taken at night with a flash, which accounts for the unusual lighting. This shows the mortar tube at maximum elevation.

A detail view from a technical intelligence report showing the internal breech of the Raketenwerfer 61 mortar.

A detail view from an American intelligence report showing the 380mm Sprenggranat 4581 rocket-propelled projectile fired from the Sturmtiger. This projectile weighed 760 pounds and had a range of 3.5 miles.

The rocket-assisted projectile was so heavy that the Sturmtiger was provided with a small crane on the right rear corner of the superstructure to reload its ammunition.

Support units of the 10th Armored Division including elements of a field artillery and antiaircraft artillery battalion prepare slit trenches for a nighttime bivouac near Trier, Germany, on 27 February. In the background are an M15A1 combination gun motor carriage, an M16 machine-gun motor carriage, an M3A1 half-track, and several M7 105mm howitzer motor carriages.

Captured near Rath castle on 25 February, a StuG III displayes eyes and a mouth painted on the Saukopf mantlet.

An M5A1 in Rheindahlen, Germany, on 27 February during Operation Grenade. It has tactical number 72 painted on the hull side and provides a good example of the extensive stowage often carried at this stage of the war.

A jeep passes an abandoned Bergepanzer III near Rheindahlen on 27 February. The Bergepanzer III was a turretless recovery version of the Pz.Kpfw. III tank.

A column of tanks from Company C, 740th Tank Battalion, rests alongside a row of buildings in Bergerhausen on 28 February during Grenade. The lead tank, an M4A3 (76mm) commanded by Lt. Charlie Loopey of the 3rd Platoon, has a curious collection of iron scrap on the hull side and turret, which was a local effort for added protection against panzerfausts.

An M4A1 dozer tank cleans up wreckage in a village during the February fighting. An M4A3 (76mm) can be seen in the background.

An armored bulldozer is used to clear away rubble in the wake of the fighting on 28 February. Engineer units frequently followed in the path of combat units to ensure that vital roads through damaged towns were clear for supporting truck traffic.

Another view of an engineer armored bulldozer at work.

An M5A1 light tank of the 66th Armored Regiment, 2nd Armored Division, near Priestrath on 28 February prior to the attack across the Cologne plain toward the Nord Canal the following day. The tank is fitted with the usual sandbag armor on the hull front and is from the late-production batch with the cover over the folding pintle mount for the .30-caliber machine gun on the turret side.
UNITED STATES MILITARY ACADEMY

Company H, 67th Armored Regiment, 2nd Armored Division, passes through Priesterath, Germany, on 28 February on the way to the Rhine. This M4 is heavily decked in artillery camouflage net over the sandbag appliqué armor. With ground conditions drying, the tanks are returning to the use of the T51 rubber block track, but fitted with duckbill extenders.

A rear view of the column seen above showing the typical heavy stowage on the rear deck.

A column from Company G, 16th Infantry, 1st Infantry Division, in Vettweiss on 28 February during Operation Grenade. The M2 half-track, named *Public Zoo*, is from the regimental antitank company and is towing an 57mm antitank gun.

Riflemen of the 83rd Division mount up on M4 tanks of the 2nd Armored Division during operations on 28 February.

A StuG III knocked out during fighting with Patton's Third Army on 27 February near Bitburg. The hit on the assault gun's *Schurzen* side skirts is probably from a large-caliber weapon such as a 105mm howitzer.

A scene of devastation along the Our River near Dasburg following the fighting with Patton's Third Army. In the foreground is the wreck of a Bergepanther tank-recovery vehicle while behind it is a StuG III assault gun.

M4A3 (76mm) tanks and M18 tank destroyers of the 6th Armored Division near Kosheid, Germany, on the approaches to the Prum River on 28 February. In the tree line is an abandoned German King Tiger tank.

Artillery played an unusually important role in the Rhine fighting since the German artillery units were in far better condition than the decimated infantry. Some German artillery was motorized, such as this 105mm leFH 18/40 light field howitzer being towed by an RSO tracked prime mover. The dwindling supply of fuel led to the loss of many weapons like this one, captured by the U.S. Army on the west bank of the Rhine on 28 February during Operation Lumberjack.

An M4A3 of the 774th Tank Battalion passes by some riflemen of the 78th Division during the operations around Nideggen on 28 February.

Reinforcements continued to arrive in Europe. This is an M4A1 (76mm) of Company A, 20th Tank Battalion, 20th Armored Division, being prepared by its crew near Cailly in France on 24 February. The division began arriving in France on 17 February and entered combat in Germany in early April.

The crew of a late-production M4A3 with the all-vision commander's cupola from the 745th Tank Battalion watches as a rifle company from the 1st Infantry Division passes by during the operations near Suller on 27 February.

CHAPTER 4

Over the Rhine

WITH THE SUCCESS of the U.S. Ninth Army's Operation Grenade in the north, the U.S. First Army's Operation Lumberjack began on 1 March 1945 with the intention of clearing the western bank of the Rhine from the Cologne area south, linking up with the U.S. Third Army on the Ahr River near Koblenz. There were no plans to cross the Rhine in this sector, as that was scheduled to occur in the British sector around Wesel later in March. On 7 March, T26E3 Pershing tanks of the U.S. 9th Armored Division discovered that the Ludendorff Bridge over the Rhine at Remagen had not been demolished like all the other major Rhine bridges and quickly captured it to everyone's surprise.

This sudden windfall created a major change in plans for the ensuing operations into Germany. Gen. Omar Bradley proposed a new scheme, Operation Voyage, to link up the First and Third Armies on the eastern bank of the Rhine, then strike to the northeast to create a southern pincer around the Ruhr to complement Montgomery's Rhine attack near Wesel. In the meantime, Gen. Jacob Devers's 6th Army Group had already initiated Operation Undertone, an attack up along the west bank of the Rhine to undermine German defenses in front of Gen. George Patton's Third Army. This succeeded more quickly than expected, and Patton launched his army into the Saar-Palatinate, overwhelming the German defenses so quickly that the offensive was dubbed the "Rhine rat race." With Montgomery's Operation Plunder scheduled to begin on 24 March, Patton made it a point to put a division across the Rhine at Oppenheim on the night of 22–23 March, tweaking his former rival with a boast that his army had managed to cross the Rhine without artillery or any other heavy support.

With the German defenses along the Rhine on the verge of a rout, Montgomery staged the elephantine airborne-amphibious Operation Plunder near Wesel on 24 March, and Eisenhower gave Bradley permission to explode out of the Remagen bridgehead with Operation Voyage on the twenty-fifth. The rapid success of Voyage prompted Eisenhower to place the final battle for the Ruhr in Bradley's hands, with Gen. William Simpson's U.S. Ninth Army closing around the industrial zone from the north and Gen. Courtney Hodges's U.S. First Army from the south. Trapped inside was nearly the entire German Army Group B, the largest concentration of German forces on the western front.

Three M10 3-inch gun motor carriage tank destroyers advance through Münchengladbach on 1 March when the town was captured by the 29th Division during Operation Grenade, the assault over the Roer River.

A M4A1 (76mm) of the 2nd Armored Division passes through Münchengladbach on 1 March as the Roer offensive finally succeeds. This is probably one of the M4A1 tanks first used in Operation Cobra in July 1944. It has been retrofitted with the usual Ninth Army appliqué consisting of steel tank tracks, a layer of sand bags, and a covering of artillery camouflage netting over the glacis plate for added protection against panzerfausts.

A platoon of brand-new M4A3E8 tanks of the 745th Tank Battalion moves forward on 1 March while in support of the 1st Infantry Division.

Infantry of the 1st Infantry Division prepare to board M10 3-inch gun motor carriages of the 634th Tank Destroyer Battalion in Gladbach on 1 March.

One of the most common type of obstacles erected as part of the West-Stellung program was the *Panzersperre*, a log obstruction erected to block roads through towns and villages. Here an M4A3 (76mm) of the 745th Tank Battalion moves through a *Panzersperre* in Gladbach after troops have removed the center portion.

An M4A1 of the 745th Tank Battalion moves through Kelz on 1 March during Grenade.

A column of M36 90mm gun motor carriages of the 628th Tank Destroyer Battalion takes a breather in the streets of Rheydt on 1 March during the 5th Armored Division's fight to cross the Niers Canal. The lead vehicle is fitted with an armored parapet around the open turret, a frequent local improvisation in the final months of the war to protect this vulnerable area from snipers.

On 1 March, the 83rd Division prepared a small task force consisting of the 330th Infantry and tank support from the 736th Tank Battalion to sieze a bridge over the Rhine at Oberkassel near Düsseldorf. The lead element of the task force consisted of German-speaking GIs and a few tanks painted in German markings. This is one of those vehicles, an M5A1 light tank, photographed near Rheindahlen in late February. In the event, the ruse failed, and the Germans destroyed the bridge.

Tanks of the 5th Armored Division form up in the outskirts of Rheindahlen, Germany, on 1 March. The jeep in the foreground has had improvised mud guards added on either side.

An M4A3 (76mm) of the 750th Tank Battalion in Quadrath, Germany, on 2 March, the day after it was captured by the 104th Division.

A column of M5A1 light tanks of the 2nd Armored Division passes through Krefeld on 3 March. The logs on the hull side were used for helping to extract the tank from the thick mud that was a constant problem in the Roer fighting.

An M5A1 of the 102nd Cavalry Reconaissance Squadron passes a jeep on the outskirts of Heimbach on 3 March. Curiously enough, the M5A1 still has its Culin hedgerow cutter from the Normandy campaign.

An M24 light tank and jeep of the 2nd Armored Division ambushed during the fighting for Krefeld on 3 March. A penetration can be seen on the turret of the M24, behind the white star.

The new T26E3 medium tanks, later called the M26 Pershing, began arriving on the battlefront in March. This is a view of a T26E3 from the platoon of Lt. John Grimball, Company A, 14th Tank Battalion, 9th Armored Division, on the road between Thum and Ginnick on 1 March shortly before the Remagen operation. In the background is a T5E1 armored recovery vehicle pushing a set of T1E1 mine exploders.

Another view of the platoon of Lt. John Grimball near Vettweiss, Germany. It took part in the capture of the bridge at Remagen a week later on 7 March.

An M8 light armored car of a cavalry recon squadron of the Ninth Army moves through a row of antitank obstacles near Venlo in the Netherlands on 2 March. It is fitted with the usual field-improvised ring mount for a .50-caliber machine gun over the turret.

Two of the new M24 light tanks of the 4th Cavalry Group prepare for a mission near Bedburg on 2 March. The riflemen on the tank to the left are probably from an attached infantry unit as the cavalry squadrons were usually armed with M1 carbines rather than M1 rifles.

The commander of an M5A1 of Company D, 34th Tank Battalion, 5th Armored Division, blazes away at an unseen target with the tank's .30-caliber light machine in the town of Viersen on 2 March. The town had been heavily damaged by air attacks before Operation Grenade. The commander is wearing a French armored crewman's helmet; the American tanker's helmet offered no ballistic protection, and the U.S. Army made a short-lived attempt to collect old French 1940 helmets in the autumn of 1944 to remedy this situation. In the event, only a few hundred were issued, mainly to the 3rd and 5th Armored Divisions.

A column from the 5th Armored Division passes through Hardt on 2 March with an M36 90mm gun motor carriage tank destroyer evident on the left and an M3 half-track to the right.

Troops of the 4th Cavlary Reconnaissance Squadron (Mechanized), 4th Cavalry Group, inspect a Panther Ausf. A knocked out during the fighting in Flasch on 2 March.

An M4A3 (76mm) of the 10th Armored Division moves into Trier on 2 March. The Moselle River city had fallen to Patton's Third Army the night before. Its capture was a key step in Patton's drive into the Saar and across the Rhine later in the month.

An M4A3 of the 10th Armored Division covers the Adolf Hitler Platz in Trier following its capture by the Third Army.

A column from the 10th Armored Division in Trier on 3 March as Patton's Third Army began its push in the Saar. The tank behind the building to the left is one of the rare M4A3E2 assault tanks.

An M4 Calliope of the 702nd Tank Battalion crosses a treadway bridge near Alsdorf, Germany, on 2 March.

This M5A1 light tank of the 701st Tank Battalion at Krefeld with the 102nd Division on 2 March is a good example of the final-production configuration with the added rear stowage bin and the late-pattern wheels.

An M36 90mm gun motor carriage of the 771st Tank Destroyer Battalion stands guard at a roadblock in Krefeld while an M4A3 (76mm) of the 701st Tank Battalion passes by in the background. Both units were supporting the 102nd Division at the time.

A pair of tanks from the 2nd Armored Division in Krefeld on 3 March during the advance on the Rhine. A large amount of armor was sent through the town as the positions on the opposite side of the Rhine were held by the Panzer Lehr Division.

This Panther Ausf. G was found abandoned in Krefeld on 3 March after the fighting for the nearby Rhine bridge by the 2nd Armored Division. It is a rare example of one of the Panthers fitted for infrared night-fighting equipment. Careful inspection of the right hull rear shows where the infrared equipment box was fitted, though it is missing in this photo.

A column of well-camouflaged M4A3 tanks of the 2nd Armored Division moves through Krefeld on 2 March during the assault toward the Rhine. Curiously enough, the second tank in the column is still fitted with a Culin hedgerow cutter.

An M4A3 fitted with an M1 dozer leads a column from the 36th Tank Battalion, 8th Armored Division, near Merbeck, Germany, on 2 March. It is probably being used to support the divisional engineer unit behind it. In the background is a knocked-out and burned Sherman. This bulldozer tank has its unit identification codes painted on the M34A1 gun mount instead of the usual location on the transmission housing.

Antitank ditches were a major problem when attacking the West-Stellung defenses. One of the more prevalent improvisations for this task was to adapt the M31 tank-recovery vehicle to lay a length of treadway bridge over the gap. This example is interesting in that the turret has been removed and a new jib crane has been installed by the 6638th Engineer Mine Clearing Company. It is being tested near Badonviller on 3 March. The 6638th Engineer Mine Clearing Company was the jack-of-all-trades specialist armor unit of the Seventh Army.

Here the bridgelayer devised by the 6638th Engineer Mine Clearing Company is seen moving over the treadway bridge that it has just laid over the antitank ditch.

A front view of the M31 after it has laid the treadway bridge.

This is a close-up view of the attachment fitted to the front of an M31 treadway bridge launcher near Badonviller, France, on 3 March. Note that the M31 is turretless.

HQ Company of the 736th Tank Battalion prepares 105mm ammunition for its M4 (105mm) assault guns while supporting the 83rd Division near Neuss, Germany, on 3 March. The ammunition came packed in the fiberboard tubular containers seen on the ground.

An M3A1 half-track of the 61st Armored Infantry Battalion, 10th Armored Division, advances in Germany on 3 March.

Wehrmacht POWs watch as a column from the 6th Armored Division advances along the highway near Giesen on 3 March.

A T34 Calliope on an M4 composite-hull tank named *Annabelle* of Company A, 48th Tank Battalion, 12th Armored Division, near Obermodern, France, on 3 March. It is fitted with the characteristic sandbag appliqué armor racks so typical of the tank units of the Seventh Army, including the 12th Armored.

An M24 light tank of the 8th Armored Division supports infantry from the 35th Division in the fighting around Lindforth on 6 March. Having replaced nearly all their old M5A1 light tanks, this division had an unusually large number of new M24 light tanks on hand—nearly seventy in service.

Troops of the 8th Armored Division look over an M24 of Company D, 36th Tank Battalion, knocked out during the fighting around Lindfort. The kneeling soldier is pointing to a penetration in the lower hull while the soldier in the background points to a hit on the hull side.

A view of the other side of the knocked-out M24 in Lindfort on 9 March. Although well armed compared to the older M5A1, the M24 had modest armor that offered protection only from small arms and machine guns.

A column of M24 light tanks of the 8th Armored Division knocked out during the fighting on the outskirts of Rheinberg on 5 March. The 36th Tank Battalion was advancing across open ground between Lindfort and Rheinberg when hit by a volley of rounds from German antitank guns.

A view inside Rheinberg following the fighting with three M4A3 tanks of the 36th Tank Battalion.

Riflemen walk by a disabled M24 of the 8th Armored Division in the outskirts of Lindfort on 6 March. The fighting for Lindfort and Rheinberg by Combat Command B of the 8th Armored Division cost the division forty-one tanks, hit mainly by German antitank guns.

A column of M4A3 and M4A3 (76mm) tanks of Company B, 36th Tank Battalion, 8th Armored Division, await further instructions in Rheinberg on 6 March.

Troops of the 2nd Infantry Division ride on M4A3 tanks of the 756th Tank Battalion in the town of Harscheid on 8 March.

An M24 light tank advances through a German city in March, with a destroyed German 37mm PaK 36 antitank gun in the foreground.

The self-propelled M16 machine-gun motor carriage antiaircraft half-track has been the primary focus of coverage here, but another common version of the quadruple .50-caliber mount was the M51 quad .50-caliber machine gun on trailer mount as seen here during the defense along the Rhine near Remagen in March.

The 38th Cavalry Reconnaissance Squadron is seen on the streets of Altenahr on 9 March. Two of the unit's M5A1 light tanks can be seen on the right along with an armored jeep and German truck, while to the left are some of the squadron's M8 light armored cars.

GIs of the 35th Division inspect a 150mm Kanone 39 in Rheinberg on 10 March during the fighting along the Roer River. This was a rare find as the Kanone 39 was originally built by Krupp for a Turkish order, and much of the production run was diverted to coastal defense.

The crew of an M4A3 tank from the 48th Tank Battalion, 12th Armored Division, loads 4.5-inch rockets into the T34 launcher during test-firing near Obermorden, France, on 3 March. This view shows many of the features added to the 12th Armored Division tanks, including the sandbag appliqué armor on the hull side.

A Calliope rocket tank of the 10th Armored Division seen in a woods in the Saar on 18 March during the advance of Patton's Third Army.

A dramatic view as an M4 with T34 Calliope of the 40th Tank Battalion, 14th Armored Division, fires a rocket salvo over the Moder River near Obermorden on 3 March. These operations proceeded the attack into Germany on 15 March.

A T34 Calliope launcher on a heavily sandbagged Sherman of the 14th Armored Division in Alsace in March.

A U.S. Army M25 tank-transporter truck trailer is used to move a British Sherman 17-pounder Firefly in the Ninth Army sector on the Meuse on 3 March during the preparations for Operation Plunder, the British assault over the Rhine.

Crew members of an M5A1 light tank of the 5th Armored Division perform household chores on their tank during a lull in the fighting near Sevelen on 4 March to the west of the Essen industrial belt. The vehicle carries a tactical "speed" number of D-16 and a pin-up cartoon to the left of the star.

Two M5A1's of the 3rd Armored Division push forward on a muddy road on the outskirts of Cologne on 4 March while curious civilians look on. The tank to the right has a large field-expedient stowage bin added to the rear.

A GI advances cautiously on a burning StuG III Ausf. G that has been knocked out in combat with the 5th Armored Division during the fighting on 4 March near Repelen on the outskirts of the Essen industrial belt.

A curious photo of a dozer tank of the 66th Armored Regiment, 2nd Armored Division, with two large holes blown in the blade. Many units used dozer tanks to lead columns if M4A3E2 Jumbo assault tanks were not available, since the dozer offered a measure of stand-off protection against ambushes by German panzerfaust antitank rockets.

Although two T26E3's were knocked out in the fighting on the approaches to Cologne, only one was a complete loss, this tank (serial number 25) from Company H, 33rd Armored Regiment, 3rd Armored Division. It was hit at point-blank range of about 200 yards by an 88mm round from a Nashorn self-propelled tank destroyer, which penetrated the lower bow armor under the transmission, setting off the ammunition in the floor. The round passed between the driver's legs, but surprisingly, the entire crew survived.

A close-up of the battle damage on this Pershing from the 88mm hit.

A pair of StuG III assault guns knocked out during the fighting near Modrath in the Cologne area in March. They are from the later-production batches with the cast *Saukopf* gun mantlet.

This is the M4A3E8 command tank of Col. Creighton Abrams of the 4th Armored Division in March. Like many tanks of Patton's Third Army, it has been retrofitted with added armor on the hull front, hull sides, and turret. This is Abrams's third Sherman tank in the European theater; it is named *Thunderbolt VII*, as can be seen on the side appliqué armor.

This view of Abrams's M4A3E8 gives a better glimpse of the turret armor. Abrams crew also mounted a .30-caliber machine gun on the cover over the gunner's sight.

This is a column of M4 medium tanks from the 745th Tank Battalion led by an M4A3 (76mm) supporting the 1st Infantry Division on 5 March.

The commander of the 4th Armored Division, Maj. Gen. Hugh Gaffey (center), conducts an impromptu planning session with the officers of the 53rd Armored Infantry Battalion in the woods near Ginsdorf on 5 March. The M4A3 (76mm) in the foreground is fitted with a slab of appliqué armor on the side.

Troops of the 145th Armored Signals Company of the 9th Armored Division lay field telephone wire from an M2A1 half-track and jeep in Euskirchen on 5 March.

An M36 90mm gun motor carriage of the 803rd Tank Destroyer Battalion waits for further instructions while supporting the 5th Infantry Division near Gorpdorf on 5 March. Behind the tank destroyer can be seen a typical *Panzersperre* antitank barrier at the end of the road.

An M4A1 of the 750th Tank Battalion moves forward in support of the 104th Division in the rubble of Cologne on 6 March.

This T26E3 (serial number 36) from Company D, 32nd Armored Regiment, 3rd Armored Division, was one of the first Pershings to see combat. It is seen here advancing down a street in Cologne on 6 March.

GIs of the 104th Division take cover in the ruins of a post office in Cologne as an M4A3 105mm assault gun of the 750th Tank Battalion advances down the rubble-strewn streets.

A later photo from the sequence showing the Pershing advancing under an overpass in Cologne.

Here the T26E3 is seen on the streets of Cologne during the fighting on 6 March, with a spent 90mm propellant casing being tossed out the shell-ejection port. This particular tank was credited with knocking out two Tiger I tanks during the battles around Cologne.

Infantry accompany a pair of M4A1 (76mm)'s of the 3rd Armored Division on the streets of Cologne.

GIs hunker down behind an M4A3 (76mm) on the approaches to Cologne cathedral on 6 March. The attack on the city included tank units from the 3rd Armored Division as well as infantry-support units like the 750th Tank Battalion with the 104th Division.

A column of medium tanks from the 3rd Armored Division moving toward the cathedral in Cologne.

An 88mm flak gun on the simplified *Behelfskreuzlafette* mounting that took part in the fighting for the Cologne bridgehead in March.

An M4A3 of the 3rd Armored Division passes a demolished tram car in Cologne.

GIs accompanied by an M4A1 tank move through the ruins of Cologne on 6 March.

During the fighting in Cologne, a Panther Ausf. A tank of the 2nd Battalion, Panzer Regiment 33, 9th Panzer Division, took up a position in front of the cathedral. This still image from some motion-picture film shows the crew of the two M4A3 abandoning their tanks after having been hit by the Panther in front of the cathedral.

The Panther was subsequently engaged by a T26E3 commanded by Sgt. Bob Early from Company E, 32nd Armored Regiment, 3rd Armored Division, that charged the Panther from the side. The Panther was still slowly turning its turret toward its opponents when the first of three rounds slammed into the tank

This overhead view shows the Panther in the cathedral square below.

This is a close-up view of the Cologne Panther a few days after the battle in front of the cathedral.

An M4A3E2 assault tank of the 3rd Armored Division moves through the ruins of Cologne on 6 March. This is one of about 100 M4A3E2 assault tanks that were rearmed with 76mm guns in February by 12th Army Group ordnance units.

An M36 90mm tank destroyer of the 703rd Tank Destroyer Battalion searches for targets in the ruins of Cologne on 6 March. It is fitted with duckbill extended end connectors, and the lower hull has been cut away to fit these.

A column of M4A3 tanks of the 748th Tank Battalion pass by a knocked-out StuG III assault gun in Replen, Germany, on 6 March while supporting the 35th Division.

An M4A3 with an E4-5 flamethrower of the 14th Armored Division is seen moments after firing a flame burst against a German barn on 6 March.

An tank column of the 9th Armored Division prepares to move forward from Klembulleshaim on 6 March. The weather during early March was rainy and overcast, which limited the amount of close air support available to American forces.

Two M5A1's pass through a destroyed factory in the outskirts of Bad Godesberg on 7 March. They are probably from the 746th Tank Battalion, which was supporting the 9th Infantry Division in its attempts to capture the town that day during the push to the Rhine alongside the neighboring 9th Armored Division.

Tanks from the 9th Armored Division pass through Carsweiler on their way to the Rhine on 7 March. The tank in the lead is an M4A3 (76mm).

An M4 medium tank of the 701st Tank Battalion is seen in the left foreground as an M7 105mm howitzer motor carriage of Company A, 73rd Armored Field Artillery Battalion, 9th Armored Division, passes through Hottorf on 6 March.

An M18 76mm gun motor carriage of the 656th Tank Destroyer Battalion carries infantry of the 9th Armored Division during the fighting on the approaches to the Rhine on 7 March near Lautershofen.

On 7 March, Task Force Engeman of the 9th Armored Division surprised the German defenders of the Ludendorff Bridge at Remagen and seized the Rhine crossing after the demolition charges failed. The attack was led by Lt. John Grimball's platoon of four T26E3 tanks of the 14th Tank Battalion, 9th Armored Division, including this one, photographed in the town a few days later.

After engineers reinforced the damaged Ludendorff Bridge, M4A3 tanks of 14th Tank Battalion, 9th Armored Division, were sent over it on 8 March to reinforce the bridgehead. Troops are seen passing by the two eastern towers that had housed machine-gun positions for the defense of the bridge. U.S. ARMY

The new T26E3 Pershing tanks of Grimball's platoon were too heavy to risk moving across the damaged Ludendorff bridge, so on 12 March, they were ferried across the Rhine.

The first air-defense unit to reach the Ludendorff Bridge at Remagen after its capture on 7 March was Battery A, 482nd Anti-Aircraft Artillery Automatic Weapons Battalion (Self-propelled), attached to the 9th Armored Division. The second platoon moved to the east bank of the Rhine early on 8 March, but the remainder of the battery stayed on the west bank to provide air cover.

Another view of M16 half-tracks of the 482nd Anti-Aircraft Artillery Automatic Weapons Battalion (Self-propelled) covering the Ludendorff Bridge at Remagen following its capture. This battalion claimed twenty-one German aircraft in the subsequent fighting around the bridge.

A reconnaissance unit of the 9th Armored Division passes through Remagen. The Nazi party stepped up its propaganda efforts in the final months of the war; the slogan on the wall reads, "Those listening to enemy radio and rumor mongers are traitors to the nation and are as good as dead."

A squad of infantry from the 99th
Division rides on the back of an M4A3 of
the 786th Tank Battalion during the
efforts to reinforce the Remagen
bridgehead. It carries corduroy matting
on the hull side, and the tracks are fitted
with extended end connectors.

Infantrymen of the 78th Division ride on
tanks of the 741st Tank Battalion through
the streets of Remagen on 9 March
during the efforts to reinforce the
bridgehead.

A Patterson-mount half-track deployed
for defense along the Rhine during the
defense of the Remagen bridgehead on
14 March. The Patterson conversions
combined towed quad .50-caliber
machine-gun mounts with surplus M2
half-tracks to create an expedient version
of the M16 machine-gun motor carriage.

A pair of 540mm tracked super-heavy mortars of Karl-Batterie 638 were used to bombard the Remagen bridge, and Karl-Gerät Nr. V *Loki* is seen on its rail transport in April after it was captured by the U.S. Army. NARA

This damaged M36 tank destroyer was converted into a tracked prime mover by the 24th Armored Engineer Battalion with the addition of a sheet-metal weather cover complete with a jeep windshield.

Another view of the improvised prime mover in use by the 4th Armored Division towing a trailer with an armored bulldozer near Kyll, Germany, on 7 March during operations along the Rhine. There was a custom-built analog of this, the M35, based on surplus M10 tank destroyer hulls, which was used by heavy artillery units for towing.

An M36 90mm gun motor carriage of the 899th Tank Destroyer Battalion stands as a road block on the rain-soaked streets of Bad Godesberg, Germany, on 7 March. The city was spared artillery bombardment because of the large number of hospitals located there.

A wrecker truck from the service company of the 275th Armored Field Artillery Battalion lowers the 105mm howitzer of an M7 105mm howitzer motor carriage into place during repair work near Nieukerk on 7 March. It is named *Merry Widow* and displays a small cartoon to the left of the star. The vehicle is a late-1944 production type with the improved sponson stowage box and basket. This battalion converted from towed to self-propelled artillery in February—hence the newer version of the M7 105mm howitzer motor carriage.

Troops of the 11th Infantry, 5th Division, use some captured German Sd.Kfz. 251 Ausf. D half-tracks moving through Trier on 7 March a week after the city had fallen. Judging from the vehicle nearby, they might be part of the division's 5th Recon Troop.

An unidentified armored infantry battalion collects German prisoners during the March fighting. Behind them is a StuG III assault gun and an American half-track.

An M4 of the 7th Armored Division on a street in Bad Godesberg on 10 March. The tank is covered with Sommerfield matting that was used to attach camouflage.

A column of medium tanks of the 40th Tank Battalion, 7th Armored Division, passes through Neidersorpe on 8 March.

This M4 tank of the 701st Tank Battalion was hit four times by German antitank guns during the fighting near Hottorf on 6 March while supporting the 102nd Division.

An M8 light armored car and bantam from a cavalry recon squadron of the U.S. Ninth Army stop in the town square of Moers on 8 March. The town had been captured on 5 March by the 84th Division, but like many Rhine towns, the bridge across the river had already been demolished by retreating German troops.

M4A1 tanks of the 702nd Tank Battalion supporting the 76th Infantry Division advance through the fields outside Binsfield, Germany, during the Third Army's attack on the town on 8 March. To the left of the Sherman is an M32 armored recovery vehicle.

GIs of the 39th Infantry, 9th Infantry Division, mount up on tanks of the 746th Tank Battalion during the advance near Bad Godesburg on 8 March, part of the effort by the division to clear the Rhine south out of the Bonn area.

Operation Undertone was aimed at breaking through the German fortified border defenses to close on the lower Rhine. Here a GI of the 94th Division walks through a gap in a road block in Lampaden past an M4A3 (76mm) of the 778th Tank Battalion that has been knocked out by two gun penetrations through the transmission cover during the fighting for the Saarbrücken bridgehead by the Third Army on 9 March.

An emplaced 88mm flak gun captured during the fighting in the Ninth Army's sector near Neuss on 9 March. These flak positions were often used for antitank defense during the final battles in Germany.

A column from the 10th Armored Division, including this M4A3E8 tank, passes through Issel on 9 March during the attacks by Patton's Third Army in the Saar-Palatinate.

Task Force Van Houton from Combat Command B, 2nd Armored Division, was given a rough reception during the fighting for Rheinberg on the west bank of the Rhine on 9 March. German antitank guns and panzerfausts knocked out thirty-nine of the fifty-four tanks used in the attack. This M4A3 took five hits, one of them completely shearing off the left drive sprocket.

Crews from the 2nd Armored Division try to pry open the hatch to free a wounded crewman from an M4A3 knocked out in the street fighting in Rheinberg. The attack was so costly because of the lack of supporting infantry and the expectation that the town would not be so heavily defended.

An ordnance unit of the 12th Armored Division mounts a T34 4.5-inch Calliope rocket launcher on an M4A3 tank named *Michigan* of the 12th Armored Division near Fletrange, France, on 9 March. At the time, the division was in reserve in the Saarbrucken area, awaiting orders to join Patton's Third Army for a push beyond the Rhine.

Another view of the Calliope—named *Cold Storage*—during the demonstration near Fletrange.

A T34 Calliope of Company B, 714th Tank Battalion, 12th Armored Division, is test-fired near Fletrange on 9 March.

An M4A1 medium tank of the 741st Tank Battalion covered with Sommerfield matting crosses a treadway bridge at Dumpelfeld, Germany, on 9 March. This was the only survivor of the original tanks that landed with the battalion at Normandy and is still fitted with a Cullin hedgerow cutter. The tank commander is wearing a French-pattern tanker's helmet.

An M5A1 of the 10th Cavalry Recon Squadron in Fohren, Germany, on 9 March. This is an interesting example of the M5A1 with extended end connectors on its tracks.

German troops from the LXVII Corps remained trapped along the Rhine south of Remagen. The pocket was finally overwhelmed on 9 March by an assault on Andernach and the neighboring towns by the 11th Armored Division, as seen here.

One of the less common assault guns was the StuG IV. This one is being recovered by an M32 tank-recovery vehicle. It has suffered an internal explosion that removed the roof and much of the engine deck.

Another example of a StuG IV, knocked out near Helfengerhoff by the 776th Tank Destroyer Battlion on 9 March. The nickname on the barrel is *Kunigunde*.

One of the new M24 light tanks of F Troop, 117th Cavalry Recon Squadron, on 9 March during training at St. Jean Saverne in France. The M24 was often more prominently marked with national insignia than the more familiar M4 medium tanks and M5A1 light tanks since there was concern that its novel shape and features would lead to it being confused with a German tank.

An armored infantry company of the 11th Armored Division in jeeps and half-tracks clogs the streets of Miesehain, Germany, on 9 March.

A Panther Ausf. A is seen burned out in front of Beethoven Hall in Bonn on 9 March.

GIs of the 16th Infantry, 1st Infantry Division, take shelter near a knocked-out Panther of Panzer Brigade 106 shortly before German troops demolished one of the last bridges over the Rhine in the city.

This T34 Calliope rocket tank of the 10th Armored Division is waiting in the woods near Losheim, Germany, on 10 March. Like many medium tanks at this stage of the war, it is fitted with sand bags for added protection and duckbill end connectors on the tracks for better mobility in mud.

An M5A1 of the 37th Tank Battalion, 4th Armored Division, passes some wreckage in the outskirts of Worms on 20 March.

An M12 155mm gun motor carriage begins to move forward to deal with a bunker while supporting the 103rd Division in Alsace during the push toward the Rhine on 20 March.

A battalion of M12 155mm gun motor carriages provides artillery fire support to the 11th Armored Division near Budesheim, Germany, on 10 March during attacks along the Rhine River. The vehicle in the foreground is named *Alberta IV*.

Two M8 light armored cars of Combat Command A, 10th Armored Division, pass through an artillery-blasted woods near Wittlich, Germany, on 10 March.

An ordnance team demonstrates a new and experimental smoke discharger to tank troops of the VI Corps on 10 March. This hull-mounted smoke-grenade launcher was not used in signficant numbers since it duplicated the role of the 2-inch turret mortar already in use.

Tankers of the 11th Armored Division use a factory in Linford, Germany, to repair their M4A3E8 tank on 11 March.

A GI inspects a hastily camouflaged Panther Ausf. G abandoned on the streets of Kehlberg on 11 March.

The new T26E3 tank was too heavy to use some of the U.S. Army's existing tactical bridging, so in many cases, they were ferried over rivers using pontoon ferries as seen here during the Rhine operations.

The effect of large-caliber artillery projectiles could be very dramatic as seen in this Pz.Kpfw. IV with its lower bow blasted open.

An M36 90mm gun motor carriage supporting the 44th Division passes through the ruins of Rimling, France, during the fighting in Alsace on 12 March.

Panzergruppe Hudel had little success in stopping the American advance out of the Remagen bridgehead. This Jagdpanther tank destroyer of the 1st Company, schwere Panzer Jäger Abteilung 654 (654th Heavy Tank Destroyer Battalion) was one of three knocked out during the fighting on 13 March near Kaimig-Ginsterhain by an M36 90mm tank destroyer.

Victor and vanquished. This Jagdpanther of the 1st Company, schwere Panzer Jäger Abteilung 654 of Kampfgruppe Paffrath, lies by the roadside as an M36 90mm tank destroyer advances past near Kaimig-Ginsterhain on 13 March. Several penetrations are evident on the rear hull side. This was one of three Jagdpanthers knocked out that day.

Another view of the Kampfgruppe Paffrath Jagdpanther being inspected by a GI.

The ground shudders when an M12 155mm gun motor carriage named *Pill-Box Annie* of the 989th Field Artillery Battalion fires point-blank at a German pillbox in the Siegfried Line near Schelbach, Germany, while supporting the 45th Division on 13 March. The M12's 155mm gun, derived from a World War I French gun, was one of the few weapons capable of penetrating the pillboxes along the Siegfried Line.

An M4 (105mm) assault gun of the headquarters platoon, 38th Armored Infantry Battalion, 7th Armored Division, during fighting along the Rhine on 13 March.

An M18 76mm gun motor carriage of the 704th Tank Destroyer Battalion, 4th Armored Division, crosses a treadway bridge over the Moselle River in Germany during the Saar-Palatinate fighting on 15 March.

American units would often put German artillery into temporary use to use up caches of German ammunition. Here an 88mm gun is used by the 95th Armored Field Artillery Battalion, 5th Armored Division, near Moers on 11 March with an ample store of ammunition in the foreground.

Here a crew from Battery B, 325th Field Artillery Battalion, fires a captured 88mm flak gun near Jerdingern on 15 March. This battalion was a standard field artillery unit using towed 105mm howitzers.

An M36 90mm gun motor carriage stands watch over a casualty while awaiting an ambulance near Guidekirch, France, on 15 March. The soldier from the 71st Infantry Regiment lost a leg to a mine. The M36 is located in a mine-cleared lane, as is evident by the white engineer's tape along the edge of the road. The M36 had duckbill end connectors fitted to its track, which gave the vehicle better flotation in muddy conditions.

The Staghound armored car was a rare example of an American-manufactured armored vehicle built in large numbers but never used by the U.S. Army. This example belongs to a column from 10 Troop, B Squadron, XII Manitoba Dragoons, supporting the II Canadian Corps in the Hochwald near Sonsbeck, Germany, in March.
PUBLIC ARCHIVES CANADA

GIs of the 301st Infantry, 94th Division, head for cover past an M36 90mm gun motor carriage as German artillery shells whistle overhead in Schillingen on 15 March 1945. The M36 was parked in the town while awaiting orders to move on Kell, Germany.

An infantry command post half-track of 12th Armored Division in Alsace.

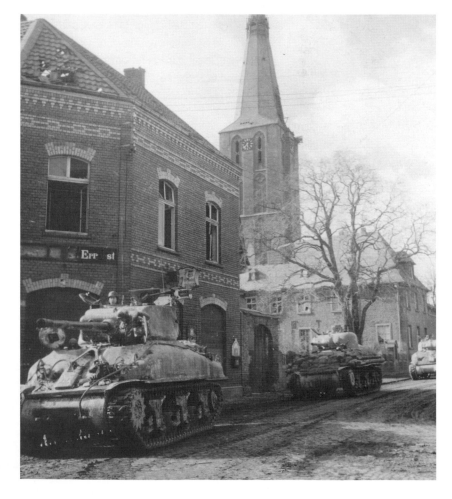

A battered old M4A1 (76mm) leads a column of tanks from the 3rd Armored Division through the town of Kerpen on 16 March on the outskirts of Cologne.

An M4A3 (76mm) of the 778th Tank Battalion rests in the ruins of Hermeskeul on 16 March while supporting the 94th Division attack.

A squad from the 394th Infantry, 99th Division, rides an M4A3 named *Beer Barrel* from Company B, 786th Tank Battalion, during operations near Hönningen on 16 March. The town fell that day after heavy combat, part of an effort to expand the Remagen bridgehead on the east bank of the Rhine.

The 14th Armored Division crossed the German border near the old fortress town of Wissembourg in Alsace on 15–16 March on the beginning of its offensive toward Neustadt. This Panzer IV/70 (V) tank destroyer was one of the first armored vehicles overcome during the attack.

An M4 tank of Company C, 735th Tank Battalion, prepares to cross the Moselle River near Kobern while supporting the 87th Division's attack toward Koblenz on 16 March. The tank crew has placed the fluorescent air-identification panel on the turret roof.

An M4 tank of the 735th Tank Battalion is ferried across the Moselle by engineers on 16 March.

A well-protected M4A3 (76mm) with horizontal volute spring suspension of the 781st Tank Battalion passes through the Alsatian fortress city of Bitche following the 100th Infantry Division's long siege, which ended on 16 March.

Crewmen of an M36 90mm gun motor carriage of Patton's Third Army reload ammunition near Sertig, Germany, on 16 March. This is ammunition being loaded into the ready racks at the rear of the turret; the ammunition stowed in the hull was left in the transport tubes.

On 17 March, two Jagdtiger heavy tank destroyers of the schwere Panzer Jäger Battalion 653 (653rd Heavy Tank Destroyer Battalion) broke down near Morsbronn-les-Bains and were abandoned by their crews. Before departing, the crews triggered demolition charges that set off the vehicle ammunition, blowing off the roof and setting fire to the vehicles. This Jagdtiger, commanded by Feldwebel Telgmann, has tactical number 332 and is being examined by GIs.

Another view of Jagdtiger 332 near Morsbronn shows the heavy cradle fitted to the front of the vehicle to lock the gun barrel in place during travel.

A First Army M16 provides cover for engineers (in the background) while they erect tactical bridging over the Rhine on 17 March, ten days after the capture of the Ludendorff Bridge in nearby Remagen. The battalion's insignia is seen painted on the side along with kill markings.

A three-quarter-ton truck of the 26th Division drives by a destroyed Jagdpanzer 38(t) during the division's attack from Saarlautern toward the Rhine with Patton's Third Army on 18 March.

An M36 90mm gun motor carriage named *Pork Chop* of the 2nd Cavalry, Third Army, takes a breather during operations in Germany on 18 March.

Engineers of the 125th Engineer Battalion, 14th Armored Division, complete work on the pilings for a bridge over the Seltzbach River near Niederroedern on 18 March, with an M3A1 half-track from the unit in the foreground.

An M32 tank-recovery vehicle assists a six-ton bridging truck in positioning a treadway bridge section during operations by the 55th Armored Engineer Battalion, 10th Armored Division, near Wedern, Germany, on 18 March.

An M25 Dragon Wagon tank transporter is seen passing over a repaired bridge on 18 March at Roermann while carrying an LVT-2 amtrac intended for use during the Rhine-crossing operations.

This M4A3 (76mm) has been modified with a layer of concrete armor on the glacis plate to provide protection against German antitank rockets and is seen here in Gelsenkirchen on 19 March.

The crew of an M4 (105mm) assault gun of the 2nd Armored Division applies finishing touches to a layer of concrete armor on the glacis plate of their tank in Gelsenkirchen on 19 March. The use of poured concrete was an alternative to sandbag armor in some units.

A disabled Panzer IV/70 (A) lies on the outskirts of Himberg on 19 March after the town was taken by the 1st Infantry Division.

Patton's "Rhine rat race" in mid-March collapsed German Army Group G's defenses in the Saar-Palatinate and opened another route to the Rhine. Here the 37th Tank Battalion of the 4th Armored Division enters Alzey, Germany, on 20 March. The M4A3 (76mm) with horizontal volute spring suspension to the right is the battalion commander's tank. The tank on the left is an M4A3E2 Jumbo assault tank that has been rearmed with a 76mm gun. The thickened side armor, glacis armor, and thickened gun mantlet are evident in this view.

An M4A3 of the 745th Tank Battalion knocked out while supporting the 1st Infantry Division during the fighting in Rottbitze on 20 March. The M4A3 is an early dry-stowage type that has been rebuilt with appliqué armor, exhaust deflector, extended fenders, and duckbills. This configuration was far less common than the wet-stowage M4A3.

An M4A3E2 Jumbo assault tank of the 37th Tank Battalion, 4th Armored Division, passes thorough Alzey on 20 March. This is a good example of an M4A3E2 rearmed with a 76mm gun,

A column from the 10th Armored Division passes through the burning remains of a German column in the outskirts of Frankenstein on 21 March, with an M4A3 medium tank in the foreground.

An M4A3 (76)W with horizontal volute spring suspension of the 41st Tank Battalion, 11th Armored Division. Named *Flat-Foot-Floogie*, it was the first tank from Patton's Third Army to reach the Rhine in Germany during the 21 March breakthrough. Careful inspection of the hull front will reveal that the tank sports a layer of appliqué steel armor.

Schwere Panzer Jäger Abteilung 653 (653rd Heavy Tank Destroyer Battalion) abandoned two of its massive Jagdtiger tank destroyers after they were damaged in fighting with the 10th Armored Division near in Neustadt an der Weinstrasse. The vehicles were photographed by U.S. Signal Corps cameramen on 21 March. The vehicle on the street opposite, tactical number 331, later ended up at Aberdeen Proving Ground.

The assistant division commander of the 10th Armored Division roars past Jagdtiger 331 in Neustadt in his armored jeep. This particular vehicle was heavily photographed for its enormous size, if for no other reason.

An interesting view of the massive breech block of the 128mm gun in the Jagdtiger.

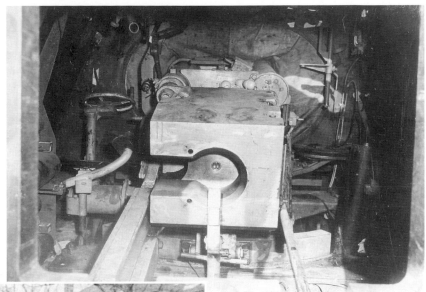

A close-up of the heavy brace used to lock the 128mm Jagdtiger barrel during transit.

The crew of a M4A3 (76mm) tank eats lunch on the streets of Leutesdorf as the division expanded its bridgehead over the eastern bank of the Rhine on 22 March. The hull is fitted with Sommerfield matting.

The Steinfeld defenses had been reinforced as part of the West-Stellung effort, with an array of antitank weapons, including pedestal-mounted antitank guns. Although most of the pedestal guns were mounted on concrete pads, some were fitted to a *Behelfslafette* improvised cruciform mount like this SK-L IIa 88mm KwK 43 of Gruppe Müller of the 5th Company of Festungs-PAK-Verband XVIII, knocked out by the U.S. 14th Armored Division near Bergzabern in the Wissembourg gap north of Steinfeld during the fighting in late March. The trunnion for this gun is completely missing.

An M8 light armored car of the 94th Cavalry Recon Squadron, 14th Armored Division, drops off a German prisoner during the fighting for the fortified Westwall town of Steinfeld on 23 March.

On 23 March, elements of the 14th Armored Division began an assault on the town of Steinfeld, a key fortified town in the Wissembourg gap providing access to the Rhine plains. This town had been heavily fortified as part of the Westwall and again in 1944–45 during the West-Stellung reinforcement. Here some M4A3 tanks of the 25th Tank Battalion load up on 75mm tank ammunition.

An M5A1 light tank of the 14th Armored Division passes by a wrecked German half-track on the road outside Berg Zabern on 23 March. The crew has added a .30-caliber light machine gun to the turret roof in a more convenient position than the usual turret side mounting.

The 9th Armored Division had most of its tanks fitted with Sommerfield matting for camouflage when first deployed in the theater in the autumn of 1944, and some of this was still in place in the spring of 1945, such as these M5A1 light tanks in Neuweid on 24 March, seen while clearing the area between the Rhine and Wied Rivers.

An M4A3E2 assault tank of the 4th Armored Division passes by a destroyed German flak truck during the fighting on the western side of the Rhine in March. Although the M4A3E2 was issued a 75mm gun, the Third Army's units replaced it with a 76mm gun beginning in February.

An M4A1 (76mm) of the 14th Armored Division moves past a roadside littered with debris from the retreating German forces near Silz, Germany, on 23 March. This tank is fitted with a .30-caliber machine gun instead of the usual .50-caliber Browning M2 HB.

Elements of the 4th Armored Division cross the Rhine on pontoon ferries near Oppenheim on 23 March as part of the breakthrough by Patton's Third Army.

Following the capture of Cologne, the 3rd Armored Division began moving some of its heavy T26E3 tanks over the Rhine using pontoon ferries.

A 3rd Armored Division T26E3 in the process of being transported over the Rhine on a pontoon ferry.

Although only in service for a few short weeks, the 3rd Armored Division's T26E3 Pershing tanks had already sprouted a variety of stowage improvisations on their hull and turret, as seen on this tank being ferried over the Rhine.

The Germans expected that the breakout from the Remagen bridgehead would take place on the northern shoulder and so placed most of their panzer strength there. This is a Panther Ausf. G of the 11th Panzer Division, knocked out during fighting with the 1st Infantry Division near Fernegierscheid during the failed counterattacks that began on 23 March.

A column of the 3rd Infantry Division, including an M36 90mm gun motor carriage of the 601st Tank Destroyer Battalion, near Bad Durkheim on 23 March.

With the expectation of crossing the Roer and Rhine, the U.S. Army began to dust off its duplex-drive amphibious tanks for possible operations. Short of the American-built M4A1 duplex-drive tanks, the U.S. Army turned to the British army for surplus duplex-drive tanks. Although not the best quality, this photo provides a rare glimpse of a depot for 736th Tank Battalion with Sherman duplex-drive tanks. The turretless duplex-drive tank second from the right is a rare U.S. Army Valentine duplex-drive tank used for training.

Another rare view, this one showing a Sherman III duplex-drive tank (M4A2) of the 736th Tank Battalion. Note the British smoke mortar fitting on the turret side and the British pattern track stowage on the hull front. This unit was one of the few American units to use the British duplex-drive tanks in combat.

Following their use at Normandy in June 1944, the U.S. Army still had about 100 M4A1 duplex-drive amphibious tanks in the European theater. They were refurbished for the Rhine crossing operation in late March. This is a training exercise by the 781st Tank Battalion near Binau on the Neckar River. This unit was attached to the Seventh Army in southern Germany and so did not participate in the Rhine crossing, although it retained its duplex-drive tanks for potential future river operations in Germany.

This is an interesting view of a duplex-drive tank of the 781st Tank Battalion showing its flotation screen completely erected. The U.S. Army ordered about 350 M4A1 duplex-drive tanks, which were converted by Firestone from M4A1's.

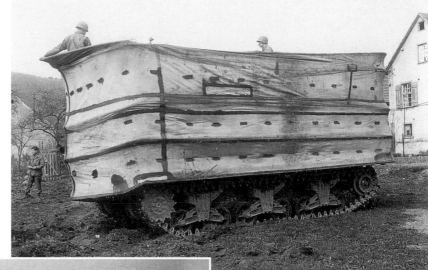

Another duplex-drive tank of the 781st Tank Battalion during a practice exercise near Binau.

A duplex-drive tank from the 781st Tank Battalion enters the water after the flotation collar has been fully erected. The propellers can be seen at the rear of the tank. The 736th Tank Battalion swam seventeen duplex-drive tanks across the Rhine on 24 March. But the 748th Tank Battalion, with fifty-one duplex-drive tanks, was able to swim only eight across the Rhine because of damage to the flotation collars during transit.

An interesting rear view of an M4A1 duplex-drive tank with Patton's Third Army near Braunshorn on 24 March during the Rhine-crossing operations showing the propellers folded up in travel position. This particular tank has extended end connectors fitted to the track and also has been modernized by the substitution of an all-around vision cupola instead of the usual split commander's hatch. Barely evident on the rear of the screen is a faded "A-8" painted on a white square. This style of marking was common on M4A1 duplex-drive tanks on D-Day, and this vehicle may very well be a survivor.

M4A1 duplex-drive tanks of the 748th Tank Battalion enter the water near Nierstein on 23 March during training for later river operations.

An M4A1 duplex-drive tank crosses a pontoon treadway bridge near Boppard on 26 March. Many of the duplex-drive tanks had damaged screens or other defects that prevented their use in an amphibious role.

An M4A1 duplex-drive tank with its screens folded passes through Durkheim during the Rhine operations on 26 March.

This duplex-drive tank of Company C, 736th Tank Battalion, was knocked out in the fighting near Frankenthal on 26 March while supporting the 30th Division. This was one of seventeen American duplex-drive tanks that crossed the Rhine on 24 March. The 748th Tank Battalion had fifty-one duplex-drive tanks for the operation, but damaged canvas screens limited the use of the tanks in an amphibious mode, and only eight actually swam across the Rhine at the end of March.

An M25 Dragon Wagon tank transporter of Patton's Third Army is seen on 27 March moving an LCM (landing craft, mechanized) up to the Rhine for the crossing operations in the Mainz-Mannheim area.

Another view of a column of M25 Dragon Wagon tank transporters being used to bring LCM's up to the Rhine for the river-crossing operations.

These M8 armored cars of the headquarters of the 104th Cavalry Recon Squadron (Mechanized) are late-production types fitted with the folding pintle mount. This feature entered production so late that it was seldom seen in the European theater. Another curious detail on these vehicles is the use of the large .50-caliber ammunition containers, usually used on antiaircraft mounts. The lead vehicle has the nickname *Pigeon of Geneva* chalked on the front mud guard. The unit was photographed at St. Nazaire, France, on 23 March.

An M36B1 of Company A, 813th Tank Destroyer Battalion, provides fire support for the 79th Division near Dinslaken along the Rhine on 24 March. This was the least common version of the M36 tank destroyer in the European theater, being based on the M4A3 hull instead of the usual M10A1 hull. This particular vehicle has an armored cover around the turret opening.

Infantry from the 30th Infantry Division mount up on M10 3-inch gun motor carriages of the 823rd Tank Destroyer Battalion during preparations for crossing the Rhine in the Ninth Army's sector on 24 March. The main push over the Rhine began the following day.

A column of M4A3 (76mm) tanks of Company A, 771st Tank Battalion, passes through Moers during the operations on 24 March.

This close-up of an M8 75mm howitzer motor carriage supporting the 66th Division near Blain, France, on 24 March gives some idea of the cramped quarters inside the turret of the vehicle. The frame in the left of the photo is the recoil guard around the 75mm howitzer breech to prevent the crew from being injured when it recoiled.

Following its lightning advance through the Saar-Palatinate triangle in mid-March, the 4th Armored Division spearheaded the attacks that seized the city of Frankfurt. Here an M4A3 of Company C, 35th Tank Battalion, 4th Armored Division, moves through the outskirts of Frankfurt on 28 March. This appears to be an old M4A3 with direct vision slots that has been rebuilt with appliqué armor and other features.

An M4A3 of the Ninth Army is gingerly driven down to the shore of the Rhine to board a pontoon ferry for the crossing on 24 March. The M4A3 has an unusual applique of steel ammunition boxes on the hull side.

Infantry wait near a heavily sandbagged M5 light tank of the 47th Tank Battalion, 14th Armored Division, during operations near Germersheim on 25 March. This is an unusual example of an old M5 with the small turret still in use in the European theater, which was far less common than the normal M5A1 light tanks and mostly seen in units that had served in the Seventh Army, which still had vehicles from the Italian campaign in its inventory.

Task Force Hunt—consisting of the 744th Light Tank Battalion, the 2nd Battalion of the 120th Infantry (30th Division), and two companies of the 823rd Tank Destroyer Battalion—attacked toward Kirchhellen at on 25 March and ran into Panzergrenadier Regiment 60 of the 116th Panzer Division. In the ensuing fight, four Sd.Kfz. 251/21 were knocked out, including the one seen here to the right (tactical number 451). The 744th Tank Battalion was unusual in that it was one of the few separate tank battalions in the European theater equipped solely with light tanks, in this case with the new M24 light tank. The battalion had fifty-one M24 light tanks on hand on 25 March.

A column of M24 light tanks of the 744th Tank Battalion support the 30th Division during fighting in the Stautsforst on 25 March.

Riflemen from the 30th Division disembark from an M24 light tank of the 744th Tank Battalion on 25 March.

The command element of a rifle platoon of the 120th Infantry, 30th Division, advances through the Wesel forest on 26 March under the watchful eye of an M24 light tank crew from the 744th Light Tank Battalion during their exploitation of the Rhine crossing.

An upgunned 76mm M4A3E2 assault tank of the 6th Armored Division is seen here burned out in a field after having been knocked out around Frankfurt on 27 March.

This early-production Pz.Kpfw. II missing its turret was found in Germany in the spring of 1945 by the Ninth Army. It was probably being used for driver training.

This burned-out Jagdpanther was knocked out in the fighting on the outskirts of Frankfurt in late March and is seen abandoned some weeks later after attempts to recover it have failed.

A pair of Panzer IV/70 (hull number 201) captured by the First Army near Oberpleis, Germany, on 25 March.

M18 76mm gun motor carriages of the 602nd Tank Destroyer Battalion move into St. Goar, Germany, in support of the 89th Infantry Division on 26 March.

An M3A1 half-track of the 26th Division moves through the ruins of Darmstadt on 26 March.

An M4A3 (76) of the 784th Tank Battalion (Colored) in operations near Dinslaken on 26 March while supporting the 35th Division.

An M18 76mm gun motor carriage of the 602nd Tank Destroyer Battalion in St. Goar engages German positions on the opposite shore of the Rhine on 26 March. A bridgehead over the river had already been secured earlier in the month when the Remagen bridge was seized.

A camouflaged M4A3 moves up toward Limburg as the 9th Armored Division expands its Rhine bridgehead beyond Remagen on 27 March.

An M2 half-track leads a truck convoy of the 89th Division through Kestert, Germany, on 27 March.

M4A3 tanks of the 11th Armored Division wait near Andernach on the west side of the Rhine as the Remagen bridgehead is expanded. They are painted with large tactical numbers on the hull side, peculiar to this unit.

An M15A1 machine-gun motor carriage antiaircraft half-track of the 482nd Anti-Aircraft Artillery Automatic Weapons Battalion of the 9th Armored Division passes through Limburg on 27 March.

An American infantryman rushes past a knocked-out King Tiger near Weverousch, Germany, on 27 March. An internal explosion has blown off the turret roof.

An M4A3 with a squad of infantry on the back moves through Weitzlar on 28 March. This is a late-production, wet-stowage M4 with the 75mm gun, a fairly common type during the 1945 campaign in Germany, though the stowage box on the hull side is unusual.

An M4A3E8 (76mm) of the 6th Armored Division guards an intersection in Offenbach on 28 March. This particular tank was one of those fitted with appliqué armor on the glacis plate, though not on the turret. It is painted with the large tactical numbers typical of the 6th Armored Division—in this case, number 28.

One of the British tanks most familiar to U.S. troops was the Churchill Crocodile flamethrower tank. Shortages of flamethrower tanks in the U.S. Army led to frequent calls for flame support from nearby British units, in this case near Sterkrade, Germany, in the Ruhr on 31 March. The Crocodile was providing support to the U.S. Ninth Army, and the plume of smoke in the background is from a massive fire at a nearby synthetic fuel plant.

An M7 105mm howitzer motor carriage of Battery C, 22nd Armored Field Artillery Battalion, 4th Armored Division, crosses a treadway bridge over the Main river near Hanau, Germany, on 28 March. This is a fairly typical example of an intermediate-production vehicle with the deepened pulpit and armored flaps, but still retaining the early suspension.

A tank column from the 8th Armored Division waits along a tree line near Kirschellen on 28 March. The tank in the foreground is an M4A3 while the other is an M4A3E8.

A GI from the 311th Infantry, 78th Division, fires at enemy troops after overrunning a German column near Honnep on 28 March 1945. The burning vehicle is an Sd.Kfz. 251/16 flame-thrower half-track, a relatively rare type.

An M4A3 (named *Ada*) of Company A, 80th Tank Battalion, advances down a road near Kirschellen on 28 March.

Troops of the 30th Division inspect a 105mm flak gun in an emplacement on 28 March. The heavy dispersion of these flak batteries became a significant tactical issue in the spring of 1945 as U.S. forces began closing in on numerous German industrial cities.

An M4A3 (76mm) of the 31st Tank Battalion, 7th Armored Division, moves into Deekenbach on 29 March with the burning wreckage of a German truck in front of it.

A new T26E3 tank test-fires its gun near Kaarst on 29 March. The 2nd Armored Division had about twenty of these new tanks in service by early April.

This M4A3 (76mm) slid into a crater caused by a massive German artillery round that struck near it in Kreul on 29 March in the Ninth Army's sector.

The initial objective of Operation Voyage was the highway at Giessen, the hinge point at which the First and Third Armies linked to begin their northward swing to Paderborn. Here an enormous column of German prisoners walks westward along the median divider as the 6th Armored Division moves to the front on 29 March. The M4A3 (76mm) with horizontal volute spring suspension to the left is fitted with additional steel armor on the glacis plate, transmission cover, and turret sides. Although kits were eventually fielded for this, many units improvised their own appliqué armor using knocked-out American and German tank hulls.

Riflemen of the 9th Infantry, 2nd Division, board tanks of the 741st Tank Battalion during operations near Giessen on 30 March.

A Panther Ausf. G tank lies burned out in the streets of Haiger on 29 March after having been knocked out by a tank from the 750th Tank Battalion, which was supporting the infantry of the 104th Division. The meager panzer force of Bayerlein's LIII Corps was unable to seriously threaten the 3rd Armored Division's advance on Paderborn.

This Jagdtiger (X7, 305058) was the first intact vehicle of this type captured by American troops and so was examined extensively by First Army technical intelligence officers. It was commanded by Lt. Sepp Tarlach and served with the 2nd Platoon of the 1st Company, schwere Panzer Jäger Abteilung 512 (512th Heavy Tank Destroyer Battalion) of schwere Panzergruppe Hudel (Heavy Panzer Group Hudel), part of the scratch German force attempting to stop the U.S. Army's exploitation of the Remagen bridgehead in late March. It was abandoned in Obernephen.

An armored reconnaissance unit of the 3rd Armored Division led by an M5A1 light tank passes through a German town south of Paderborn on 29 March.

A side view of Jagdtiger X7. This was the largest and heaviest armored vehicle to see combat in World War II, armed with a powerful 128mm gun. Heavy Panzer Group Hudel was sent into the fighting along the Sieg River during the lightning advance by the 3rd Armored Division but had little impact on the battle in spite of its imposing equipment.

A rear view of Jagdtiger X7 showing the antiaircraft mount for the MG42 machine gun in place on the back engine deck.

An LVT-4 amphibious tractor of the Ninth Army passes in front of a windmill on 29 March while carrying supplies over the Rhine during the Allied offensive.

A heavily camouflaged M4 of the 31st Tank Battalion, 7th Armored Division, passes a burning German truck during the fighting near Deckenbach on 29 March.

A camouflaged M4 of the 31st Tank Battalion, 7th Armored Division, passes through Deckenbach on 29 March.

This StuG III Ausf. G assault gun was knocked out in the fighting with the 6th Armored Division for Ziegenhahn on 30 March during its rapid drive to the Fulda River.

This Panther Ausf. G was knocked out by the 14th Armored Division near Germersheim during its advance in late March. The tank received a hit on the upper side of the turret, which shattered the armor. This is a brand-new tank as it is fitted with the small oval hooks for attaching camouflage that were only introduced on the production lines in March.

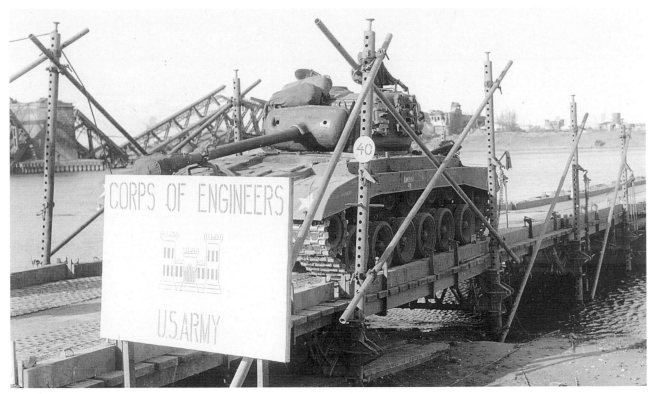

A T26E3 tank from the 3rd Armored Division crosses the Weser River on 30 March. The 3rd and 9th Armored Divisions were the first to obtain shipments of these new tanks, receiving ten each in late February.

The 3rd Armored Division column moves up to the bridge area on 30 March.

A column of T26E3 tanks that had recently arrived in the European theater are seen on their way to the Rhine River crossings on 30 March.

The T26E3 tank column is fueled up for its move to the Rhine on 30 March.

Because of the great demand for M36 tank destroyers, a small number of M36B1's were created by mating an M36 turret to an M4A3 tank hull. This example of the 11th Armored Division of Patton's Third Army passes by GIs of the 26th Division near Langensebold, Germany, on 30 March.

A platoon of M18 76mm gun motor carriages of the 705th Tank Destroyer Battalion uses a row of houses in Perl, Germany, for cover in March. The cartoon on the hull side appears to be an Indian chief in a war bonnet.

An M18 76mm gun motor carriage is used in the artillery fire support role in March. The light-colored material at the center of the vehicle is a fluorescent orange air-identification panel, commonly attached to the roofs of vehicles to prevent attacks by Allied fighter-bombers.

A heavily camouflaged M4A3 (76mm) of the 7th Armored Division passes a burned-out car on the outskirts of Haina on 30 March.

Another view of the 7th Armored Division column near Haina. It was common to mount armored infantry on the tanks to speed up the advance as seen here.

An M4A3 (76mm) of the 7th Armored Division engages a target farther down the street in Wetzlar on 28 March.

A column of M4A1 (76mm) tanks of the 7th Tank Battalion, 7th Armored Division, moves through Wetzlar.

An 88mm flak gun captured by the 771st Tank Battalion near Dulmen, Germany, on 29 March.

A column of M3A1 half-tracks of the 3rd Armored Division conduct a sniper patrol in the outskirts of Marburg, Germany, on 30 March.

An M4A1 (76mm) of the 3rd Armored Division engages targets in the outskirts of Korbach on 30 March. This tank has a number of modifications, including a large slab of armor added to the glacis and the substitution of a split hatch for the commander's usual all-vision cupola.

Ordnance troops in Patton's Third Army fuel an M4A3 (76mm) using five-gallon jerricans at a depot in Oberstein on 30 March. This is a replacement tank that is being prepared to be sent forward to a combat unit.

A jeep carrying the senior commanders of the German garrison in Hersfeld is brought back to 4th Armored Division's headquarters to negotiate surrender. Passing by is an M5A1 light tank.

A column of M5A1 light tanks of the 11th Armored Division on the approach to Frankfurt on 31 March.

An M4A3E8 tank serves as the backdrop for payday banking of the 564th Ordnance Heavy Maintenance Tank Company of the Ninth Army in Münchengladbach on 30 March. After receiving their pay, many of the men placed their earnings in the army's field banking system.

After capturing large stocks of German artillery rockets, the 370th Ordnance Battalion was tasked by the Ninth Army to create a launcher to use them up. This is their creation prior to trials on 31 March.

Another example of an improvised mount for firing captured German artillery rockets is this contraption built by the 16th Ordnance Company for the 102nd Division at Urdingen on 31 March. It consists of the carriage of a Soviet F-22 76mm field gun that had been recaptured from the Germans, with the launch frames on either side.

A field full of brand-new M4A1 (76mm) tanks at the 851st Ordnance depot at Münchengladbach at the end of March prior to being issued to tank units of the Ninth Army.

CHAPTER 5

Into Central Germany

APRIL 1945 saw the collapse of the Wehrmacht in the west. On 1 April, the Ruhr pocket was encircled by elements of the U.S. Ninth Army from the north and the U.S. First Army from the south. The Ruhr pocket contained most of Army Group B and about 325,000 German troops. With the link-up of the First and Ninth Armies at Lippstadt on Easter Sunday, 1 April, the primary focus of Gen. Omar Bradley's 12th Army Group was the Elbe River farther east. The secondary mission was the reduction of the Ruhr pocket. A new army, the Fifteenth, was brought up for occupation duty and held a line along the Rhine. Both the Ninth and First Armies left behind two corps each to gradually reduce and mop up the Ruhr pocket.

There was significant fighting during the first two weeks of the Ruhr encirclement, but German units were quickly running out of ammunition. News of the Soviet advance on Berlin and the U.S. Army's race to the Elbe made it clear to the encircled troops that the end was near. During the first two weeks of April, most American divisions surrounding the Ruhr were capturing about 500 German prisoners each day, but by 14 April, there was a dramatic change: the daily totals often reached or exceeded 2,000 by each division as Army Group B disintegrated. With the situation hopeless, Field Marshal Walter Model, Army Group B's commander, dissolved his command rather than surrender. The many underage and overage troops were simply discharged from the army on 15 April, and all noncombatant troops were allowed to surrender on the seventeenth. The German Fifteenth Army had already surrendered on 13 April and the Panzer Lehr Division on the fifteenth. The pocket largely collapsed by the eighteenth. Some 317,000 German troops surrendered in the Ruhr—a greater total than even Stalingrad or Tunisia.

The destruction of Army Group B in the Ruhr pocket marked the end of large-scale operations by the Wehrmacht in the west. The remaining forces conducted a "makeshift campaign" for the last weeks of April, a disjointed effort to conduct local defensive actions by the few divisions that had sufficient morale to continue the fight under such hopeless circumstances. The war would go on for another few weeks, but the outcome by now was obvious.

An M18 76mm gun motor carriage of the 824th Tank Destroyer Battalion provides fire support to the 2nd Battalion, 397th Infantry, 100th Division, during the capture of Wieslock on 1 April.

The 3rd Company of schwere Panzer Jäger Abteilung 512 (512th Heavy Tank Destroyer Battalion) from Panzer Group Hudel arrived in the final phase of the fighting for Paderborn, and one of its massive Jagdtiger 128mm tank destroyers was lost there on 1 April during the fighting with the 3rd Armored Division.

One outcome of the fighting in late March was the capture of the city of Kassel and, along with it, the Henschel factory where the King Tiger tank was assembled. Here a GI inspects a King Tiger turret on a railway flatcar.

An American technical intelligence team photographed this King Tiger with the early turret and a pilot Jagdtiger at the Henschel proving ground at Haustenbeck near the Henschel and Wegman plants in Kassel. The Jagdtiger is one of the two initial vehicles built with the Porsche suspension.

An overview of the tanks found at the Haustenbeck facility, including a Panther in the foreground, a King Tiger, the Jagdtiger pilot, and another King Tiger. Both King Tigers have the original type of turret.

An M8 light armored car and jeep of a cavalry reconnaissance squadron in Ahlen, Germany, on 1 April.

An M4A1 medium tank of the 709th Tank Battalion carries a load of German prisoners of war on its back deck while supporting operations of the 95th Infantry Division in Germany in April.

An M32 tank-recovery vehicle of the 5th Armored Division passes through Harsewinkel on 2 April in the wake of the fighting there.

A pair of M5A1 light tanks of the 3rd Tank Battalion, Combat Command A, 12th Armored Division, at Nassig, Germany, on 2 April. Both tanks have had their .30-caliber machine gun placed on a new pintle mount and relocated forward on the turret to make it more convenient for the crew to use without having to disembark from the turret.

A machine gunner armed with a Browning M1909A6 .30-caliber light machine gun advances behind one of the new M24 light tanks during the 1st Infantry Division's advance near Scharfenberg on 2 April.

An M4A3 (76mm) to the left and M4 to the right from the 191st Tank Battalion take targets under fire in Aschaffenburg on 2 April during the assault by the 45th Division. This town was one of the few where German civilians took an active part in the resistance along with large numbers of Hitler Youth. Rather than risk infantry, the American divisional commander shelled the town with tank and artillery fire until it finally surrendered on 3 April.

This tank graveyard near the railway yard at Aschaffenburg was photographed on 28 March. More than a dozen Panther tanks can be seen littering the repair yard.

The tank-repair yard near the Aschaffenburg railyard contained several freight cars filled with Panther tank turrets like these.

An assortment of Panther turrets left behind in the Aschaffenburg repair yard.

A view inside the panzer-repair facility at Aschaffenburg showing a line-up of panzer hulls.

The 157th Infantry Regiment, 45th Division, began house-to-house fighting for Aschaffenburg on 28 March, finally capturing the city on 3 April. During the final stage of the fighting, there was an encounter between an M36 tank destroyer of the 645th Tank Destroyer Battalion and this captured M4A3 (76mm) tank being used by the Germans. Besides the German crosses, the words *Beute panzer* ("Captured tank") were painted on the M4A3 (76mm) to prevent German troops from firing on it. It was knocked out by a 90mm hit on the glacis plate, as seen above the right headlight.

An M4A3 of the 43rd Tank Battalion, 12th Armored Division, advances through Schneeberg on 3 April carrying GIs from the 66th Infantry. The U.S. Army changed its segregation policy about blacks in the infantry in February after the Battle of the Bulge, and black volunteers served in a number of infantry divisions during the final months of the campaign.

An infantry column advances under the cover of M10 3-inch gun motor carriage tank destroyers.

The Super Pershing was based on earlier attempts in the U.S. to field a more powerful gun. This is the pilot of the T26E4 at Aberdeen Proving Ground with the new lengthened 90mm gun.

The most powerful American tank to see service in the European theater was a single Super Pershing. This was a unique test tank based on the original T26E1 pilot tank, but rearmed with the more powerful T15E1 version of the 90mm gun that was designed to offer performance comparable to the German 88mm KwK 43 on the King Tiger. It was not army practice to send prototypes into combat, but in February, ordnance decided to ship the pilot tank to the European theater for a trial by combat.

This is a view of the T26E1 pilot tank modified with the new gun with the massive equilibrator springs fitted to the roof to compensate for the barrel weight.

An overhead view of the T26E4 pilot shows the reconfiguration of the turret bustle and other changes.

The T26E4 on trials with the turret traversed to the rear. The additional length of the gun barrel required an additional counterweight at the rear of the turret for balance.

This rearview of the T26E4 pilot shows the large counterweight fitted to the rear of the turret.

The Super Pershing was assigned to the 33rd Armored Regiment, 3rd Armored Division, which by March was operating in Germany. The division's ordnance unit decided to upgrade the Super Pershing with supplementary armor to make it more equivalent to the King Tiger. No photos are known from its combat actions in April and May; this shot was taken in a tank boneyard near Kassel after the war. This tank first fired its gun in anger on 4 April, when it engaged and destroyed a German armored vehicle, possibly a Tiger or Panther, at a range of 1,500 yards during the fighting along the Weser River.

The Super Pershing ended its combat career in this tank graveyard near the Henschel Tiger plant in Kassel, surrounded by knocked-out and broken-down equipment of the 3rd Armored Division, which had fought in this area in March.

Besides requiring barrel compensators on the turret roof, the Super Pershing had a large counterweight added behind the turret to permit smooth traverse.

This other view of the Super Pershing shows the extensive added armor on the front of the turret. The large cylindrical devices on the roof are hydraulic cylinders added as equilibrators for the enormous weight of the long 90mm barrel.

The Super Pershing also had armor added to the glacis plate, as seen here. Some five tons of appliqué armor were added to the Super Pershing, including multiple layers of 40-millimeter boiler plate on the hull, a plate of 80-millimeter armor taken from a German Panther on the gun mantlet, and other scrap armor on the other locations.

A close up of the left side of the bow showing the spaced armor added to the Super Pershing's bow.

This close-up shows how two layers of 40-millimeter plate were added to the Super Pershing's bow.

A pair of heavily sandbagged M4A3 (76mm) tanks of the 771st Tank Battalion pass through the ruins of Munster on 3 April while supporting the 17th Airborne Division, which had first entered the city the previous day during the offensive over the Rhine.

Much of the fighting in the final weeks of the war was brutal house-to-house skirmishing in German towns. These two M4A3 (76mm) tanks of the 14th Armored Division were knocked out by panzerfausts, despite their sandbag armor, in the narrow streets of Lohr, Germany.

A company of tanks from the 14th Armored Division prepares to move forward in the outskirts of Lohr during the fighting there on 3 April.

An armor column from the 6th Armored Division passes the smoking remains of a German column during the advance on Oberdola and Muhlhausen. The lead tank is one of the rare M4A3E2 Jumbo assault tanks.

An M4A3E8 (76mm) of Task Force 44, 6th Armored Division, supports armored doughs of the 44th Armored Infantry Battalion during their advance into Oberdola on 4 April, part of a larger divisional operation to encircle the city of Muhlhausen.

Medics evacuate a wounded crewman from a damaged M4A3E8 (76mm) tank of the 6th Armored Division near Oberdola on 4 April. MILITARY HISTORY INSTITUTE

This sequence of photographs show infantry supported by an M4A3 (76mm) with horizontal volute spring suspension cautiously moving through Oberderla, on 4 April. In the foreground here lies an American infantryman hit by a German sniper. A BAR gunner is at the right.

In the second photo, infantry from the 6th Armored Division move past a house flying a white flag while cautiously trying to root out snipers. Although the stiffest German resistance had collapsed by April, there were still determined German soldiers who refused to surrender.

In this view, an M4A3E8 has entered an open square in Oberdola while buildings burn in the background.

The cavalry recon squadron of the 9th Armored Division occupies the town square in Pegau on 4 April while defending a bridgehead over the Diemel River. To the left is a late-production M5A1 light tank with Sommerfield matting while in the center are M8 light armored cars.

An M8 light armored car of a cavalry recon squadron of Patton's Third Army is on patrol outside Wellersen on 4 April. Not trusting the weather, the crew is still carrying snow chains on the rear engine deck.

An M4A3 (76mm) cautiously moves up behind a burning M5A1 light tank on the outskirts of Langenprozelten, Germany, during an attack by the 47th Tank Battalion, 14th Armored Division, on 4 April.

Having captured Oberdola on 4 April, the 6th Armored Division moved on to its main objective of encircling Muhlhausen. An interesting overhead view inside Muhlhausen on 5 April, the day after its capture by the 6th. An M4A3E8 (76mm) is standing guard over a number of German prisoners. It is fitted with appliqué armor over the glacis plate, a standard arrangement in the Third Army. The turret-mounted .50-caliber heavy machine gun has been supplemented by an additional .30-caliber light machine gun.

An M4A3 (76mm) with concrete armor on the glacis plate moves over a treadway pontoon bridge over the Roer on 4 April.

An M4A3E8 of the 68th Tank Battalion of the 6th Armored Division during the fighting for Muhlhausen on 5 April.

A 57mm antitank gun of an armored infantry battalion of the 6th Armored Division's Combat Command B takes up positions at a crossroads outside Muhlhausen on 8 April near an abandoned Pz.Kpfw. IV, which is a bit unusual since it is still fitted with a full set of hull skirts, which were often left off by the crews to ease maintenance.

An M4 of Combat Command B, 7th Armored Division, during the fighting around Oberkirchen on 5 April. The logs on the side were used by the crew to extricate the tank if it became stuck in mud, a common field improvisation in the wet months of the year.

Armored infantrymen of the 14th Armored Division move past an M4A3E8 (76mm) near Gemeuenden on 5 April. This tank belonged to Task Force Baum of the 4th Armored Division, which had made a daring but futile attempt to liberate a POW compound in nearby Hammelburg but which was wiped out in the process.

An M4A1 (76mm) of the 771st Tank Battalion moving through the ruins of Münster on 5 April while supporting the 17th Airborne Division. This is one of the newer-production types that appeared in the spring of 1945 and differed from the M4A1 (76mm) deployed in Normandy in having a muzzle brake on the gun, the newer turret with oval loader's hatch, and the cover over the hull air intake.

In the wake of the Rhine crossings near Wesel in late March as part of Operation Plunder, the Ninth Army continued to ferry heavy equipment over the Rhine to continue the assault on the northern side of the Ruhr. This is a shot of the operations on 6 April. LCM's (landing craft, mechanized) transport a tank destroyer battalion over the river. Here two M36 90mm gun motor carriages are moved across the river.

Here a bulldozer is used to help push the LCM back away from the shore before setting off to the east bank of the Rhine.

The cargo in this case is an M36B1, one of the least common versions of the M36 tank desrtoyer and based on an M4A3 tank chassis. This vehicle also has the parapet armor plate over the turret opening.

In this case, the vehicle being loaded aboard is the standard M36 90mm gun motor carriage, but also with the parapet armor modification over the roof opening.

This M4A3 dozer tank was used at the ferry site to help push the craft around and to grade the bank.

After the tank destroyer battalion was sent over the Rhine, a tank battalion followed, including this M4A3 (76mm).

When the LCM returned, they often brought back wounded troops or other cargo. In this case, the return trip included a medical M29C Weasel with a wounded German prisoner of war.

Another Rhine ferry site, this time using pontoon ferries instead of landing craft.

An M4A3 from the 14th Armored Division crashes over the barbed wire into the Hammelburg POW camp on 6 April. The earlier attempt by Task Force Baum of the 37th Tank Battalion, 4th Armored Division, was a bloody failure. The first attempt has been the source of controversy since it was suspected that Patton ordered the raid because his son-in-law was a prisoner in the camp.

The town crier of Anrochte is driven through the streets reading the terms of martial law from the back of an M3A1 half-track of the 8th Armored Division on 5 April. Young boys seem more curious about the affair than the adults.

An M4 of the 15th Tank Battalion, 6th Armored Division, occupies Lanensalz airbase near Muhlhausen on 6 April. In the background are some of the thirty-two German Junkers Ju 88 radar-equipped night-fighters captured at the base.

Another view of the German airfield with a new M4A3 (76mm) with horizontal volute spring suspension in the foreground.

This Jagdtiger (131) of the 1st Company of schwere Panzer Jäger Abteilung 653 (653rd Heavy Tank Destroyer Battalion) was knocked out on Heidelbergstrasse in Schwetzingen by an M4 medium tank of Combat Command B, 10th Armored Division, which hit it twice on its thinner side armor. The other two Jadgtigers of the platoon were also lost that day, one after bogging down and the other after it shed a track while retreating from the town.

An M8 light armored car of the 14th Armored Division escorts a medical convoy through Gemünden on 6 April.

A column of tanks from the 746th Tank Battalion in Olsberg on 7 April. To the left is an M4A1 and M4A3 (76mm), and to the right is an M10 3-inch gun motor carriage tank destroyer.

Gen. George S. Patton rebukes the crew of an M4A3 (76mm) for their use of sand bags on their vehicle. Patton felt that the method was not effective and that the extra weight led to premature automotive breakdowns of the tanks. This particular tank belonged to a unit that had only recently been transferred from the Seventh Army, where the sand bags were officially authorized, to Patton's Third, where sand bags were forbidden.

German prisoners are rounded up in Hesselbach on 8 April while the crew of an M4A3E8 (76mm) of the 14th Armored Division looks on. It is fitted with the usual appliqué of sand bags.

An M4A1 (76mm) of the 3rd Armored Division knocked out and burned at Blatzheim on 8 April. This veteran tank from the Normandy campaign has an alteration sometimes seen on 3rd Armored Division tanks: the switching of the vision cupola and two-piece split hatch to opposite locations on the turret roof.

An M4A3 (76mm) of the 31st Tank Battalion, 7th Armored Division, knocked out and burning during the fighting for Oberkirchen on 8 April.

A heavily sandbagged M4A3E8 of the 47th Tank Battalion, 14th Armored Division, accompanies infantry down a street in Hessenbach on 8 April.

A Jagdtiger of schwere Panzer Jäger Abteilung 512 (512th Heavy Tank Destroyer Battalion) claimed by a Sherman of the 750th Tank Battalion and seen here after it was pushed off a road near Offensen, Germany, on 9 April. An internal ammunition fire has blown off the roof.

The crew of an M4A3 (76mm) of the 781st Tank Battalion takes a breather in Heillbronn on 9 April while a bridge capable of supporting tanks was being constructed over the nearby Neckar River. This tank has the usual Seventh Army array of sand bags.

Riflemen of an armored infantry company of M3 half-tracks of the 14th Armored Division dig foxholes along the skyline in Wasserlosen on 9 April.

An M36 90mm gun motor carriage of the 814th Tank Desrtoyer Battalion, Combat Command B, 7th Armored Division, moving through Odingen on 10 April.

The headquarters company of the 786th Tank Battalion moves through Alterhundem on 10 April while supporting the 99th Division in the Ruhr pocket. The vehicle to the left is an M4A3E8 (105mm) assault gun, a relatively rare type in the European theater since few of the assault tanks with the new HVSS suspension arrived before the end of the war. This particular tank battalion was deployed in combat in late January, which probably accounts for such new equipment.

An M4A1 (76mm) provides support for the 78th Division near Honsborn on 10 April during the operations to reduce the Ruhr pocket. Aside from a few hundred M4A1 (76mm)'s issued in July 1944, this version of the Sherman tank was not widely used by the U.S. Army. In the last few months of the war, some later-production M4A1 (76mm)'s began appearing; they can be distinguished by the muzzle brake on the gun and other features.

Some of the main adversaries of U.S. Army tank units in Germany were the flak belts around the major industrial cities which had a secondary antitank use. This 128mm FlaK 40 from the unit defending the Hermann Goering Steel Works in Leuna fought a violent battle with Combat Command A, 2nd Armored Division, on 10 April before being outflanked and overrun. A single 128mm round is in the fuze setter.

An M4A3 (76mm) of the 771st Tank Battalion provides support to the 84th Division during the fighting around Hannover on 10 April.

A column from the 9th Armored Division awaits orders in a farm field outside Westhousen, Germany, on 10 April. Behind and to the right of the M4A3 is one of the new M32 armored recovery vehicles.

Infantry of the 30th Division fight their way into Braunschweig on 10 April, with the support of an M4A3E8 tank of the 743rd Tank Battalion.

An M4A3 (76mm) leads a column into Braunschweig on 11 April. The 2nd Armored Division's main opposition that day was a complex of sixty-seven large-caliber antiaircraft guns ringing the Hermann Goering steel plant southwest of the city.

An M4A3 tank of the 41st Tank Battalion, 11th Armored Division, passes a burning home in Rodach on 10 April.

Armored infantrymen of the 12th Armored Division advance with tank support in Krautostheim on 11 April. The M4A3 is from Company A, 714th Tank Battalion, and carries the unique chevron style of markings adopted by the 12th Armored Division late in the war.

An M5A1 light tank to the right and M4A3 (76mm) to the left of the 737th Tank Battalion are seen in the shadows of Greenstein castle during operations by the 5th Division on 11 April.

A column from the 4th Armored Division led by an M4 medium tank advances near Erfurt on 11 April.

An armored Infantry column of half-tracks of the 4th Armored Division heads into Jena on 11 April, with the town burning in the background.

An M10 3-inch gun motor carriage of the 644th Tank Destroyer Battalion moves down a road in Olpa on 11 April. It is still fitted with a Richardson device, a version of the Culin hedgerow cutter normally associated with the 3rd Armored Division.

An M5A1 of Company D, 761st Tank Battalion (Colored), in Coburg on 11 April.

An M2 half-track of the 759th Tank Battalion moves forward with a load of Wehrmacht prisoners on 11 April near Kalefeld.

An unusually large amount of heavy armor was employed by the Wehrmacht in the Remagen fighting because of the nearby Kassel plant, which manufactured the King Tiger. This King Tiger was captured near Mahmecke on 11 April by the 7th Armored Division during the reduction of the Ruhr pocket and belonged to either schwere Panzer Abteilung 506 of Panzer Group Hudel or schwere Panzer Abteilung 507, which supported SS Panzer Brigade Westfalen at Paderborn.

A column of M4 tanks and half-tracks of the 5th Armored Division on the move near Bismarck on 11 April.

A squad from the 17th Armored Infantry Battalion, 12th Armored Division, in Erbach on 11 April, one of a number of units partially desegregated under Eisenhower's orders in February 1945.

An M4A3E8 (76mm) of the 5th Armored Division guards a bridge on the outskirts of Tangermünde. The division pushed fifty miles on 12 April from Magdeburg but was held at the river on the outskirts of the town when the German defenders blew the bridge, leaving them only fifty-three miles from Berlin.

A King Tiger knocked out and burning near Dornholzhausen on 12 April in the First Army's sector during the Ruhr fighting.

A M7 105mm howitzer motor carriage of one of the armored field artillery battalions of the 9th Armored Division passes by some liberated French POWs near the camp at Kinderbrouck, Germany, on 12 April.

An M29C of the 255th Infantry, 63rd Division, crosses the Kocher River near Forchtenburg, Germany, on 12 April with an M20 armored utility vehicle following.

Crewmen of an M36 90mm gun motor carriage of the 818th Tank Destroyer Battalion play a game of dice behind their vehicle while waiting for a road obstacle to be cleared up ahead during operations by the 26th Division near Eisfeld on 12 April.

An M30 cargo carrier from an M12 155mm gun motor carriage battalion passes by a one-legged German World War I veteran near Westerengel, Germany, on 12 April.

GIs inspect a King Tiger of schwere Panzer Abteilung 507 that was knocked out by Task Force Kane from Combat Command A, 3rd Armored Division, in front of Hotel Kaiserhofen in the fighting in Osterode on 10 April.

A GI points out the large hole on the turret side of the King Tiger knocked out in Osterode.

A knocked-out StuG III and Jagdpanzer IV near Frenzerburg castle.

An armored bulldozer of the 237th Engineer Combat Battalion clears a burned-out King Tiger from the road near Osterode in the First Army's sector on 12 April. These two King Tigers were the last two in service with the battalion.

M3A1 half-tracks of the 6th Armored Division move across a field during a successful attempt by Patton's Third Army to drive a wedge between the German Seventh and Eleventh Armies near Lobitz on 12 April.

A fine study of armored infantry in action in the final month of the war. This is an older M3 half-track of the 46th Armored Infantry of the 5th Armored Division named *Copenhagen*, heavily encumbered with equipment, K-rations, and supplies. It is moving past a burning barn near Wittenmoor on 12 April.

An M36 90mm and M2 half-track of the 628th Tank Destroyer Battalion, 5th Armored Division, fire at German antitank rocket teams on 12 April.

A tank column of the 11th Armored Division led by an M4A3 passes through Marktzeulen on 12 April.

An M4A3 of the 781st Tank Battalion with the typical Seventh Army sandbag array while supporting the 100th Division in operations near Heillbronn on 12 April.

The 5th Armored Division reached Tangermünde on 12 April, only fifty-three miles from Berlin. Here a BAR gunner fires at targets down a street.

An M4A1 fitted with a dozer blade clears a German road obstruction in Bamberg after the town was taken by the 3rd and 45th Divisions on 13 April. This is an old M4A1 fitted with the early version of the M34 gun mount without the collars on the gun mantlet.

An M4 passes through the shattered railyard at Herzeberg on 13 April.

An M4A3E8 of the 191st Tank Battalion with the usual Seventh Army sandbag frame fires down the street in support of the 180th Infantry, 45th Division, during the fighting for Bamberg on 13 April.

A single T83 155mm gun motor carriage and a single T89 8-inch howitzer motor carriage were sent for combat trials to Europe in early 1945, taking part in the attack on Cologne with the 991st Field Artillery Battalion. The T89 pilot, seen here, had a 155mm gun tube substituted for the 8-inch tube during its combat operations in Germany. This is one of the few known combat photos of these vehicles during World War II. R. HUNNICUTT

Another of the T83/T89 pilots sent to Germany for trials with the Zebra Mission is seen in action in Germany on 30 March with the wreckage of a Ju 87 Stuka dive-bomber in the foreground.

The T83 and T89 were intended to be a family of heavy field artillery weapons. These are, to the left, one of the T89 8-inch howitzer motor carriage pilots with its shorter and stubbier barrels and, to the right, one of the T83 155mm gun motor carriage pilots. They are seen at Aberdeen Proving Ground.

This is one of the vehicles in the T89 8-inch howitzer motor carriage configuration with the 8-inch howitzer tube.

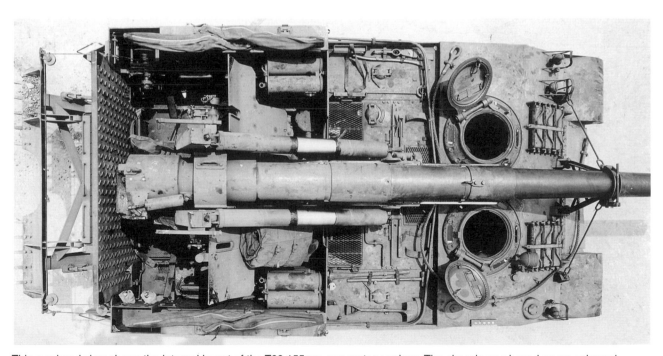

This overhead view shows the internal layout of the T83 155mm gun motor carriage. The chassis was based on an enlarged version of the M4A3E8 tank.

A rear view of one of the T83 155mm gun motor carriage pilots at Aberdeen Proving Ground. There was a large recoil spade at the rear (seen here folded down) and a work platform (above this) for the crew to service the gun.

Another rear shot of the T83 155mm gun motor carriage with a clear view of the work platform extended and the support in place.

The T83 and T89 had companion ammunition carriers. The T30 was designed to carry 102 rounds of 155mm ammunition or 66 rounds of 8-inch howitzer ammunition. It was built on the same chassis as the artillery vehicle.

A rear view of the T30 carrier. These were not ready in time for deployment to the European theater, and in the event, they were never accepted for series production because the war ended.

A Jagdtiger of the 2nd Company of schwere Panzer Jäger Abteilung 512 (512th Heavy Tank Destroyer Battalion) abandoned in Bad During after the collapse of the Ruhr pocket on 14 April. This view clearly shows the large cradle assembly used to lock down the enormous barrel of the 128mm gun while the vehicle was in transit.

A number of Sd.Kfz. 251 Ausf. D half-tracks were impressed into service by the 102nd Division following the capture of Hannover. Here they are being used to move British and American prisoners of war from a nearby camp on 14 April.

An M4A3 (76mm) of the 745th Tank Battalion engages in a street fight during the 1st Infantry Division's assault on St. Andreasberg on 14 April.

An M4A3E8 of Company A, 714th Tank Battalion, 12th Armored Division, has collapsed a small treadway bridge that had been erected over a stream near Dietersheim on 14 April.

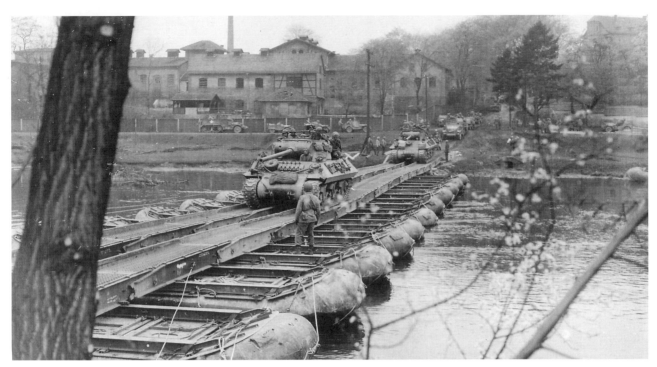

Several M36 90mm gun motor carriages of the 607th Tank Destroyer Battalion pass over a treadway pontoon bridge over the Saale River on 14 April while supporting the 87th Division.

A column of M4A3's from the 11th Armored Division moves through the rubble of Bayreuth on 15 April, a day after the city was taken by the XII Corps. The tanks are the later wet-stowage M4A3 and carry the large tactical numbers typical of the 11th Armored Division at this stage of the war.

The commander of an M18 of the 603rd Tank Destroyer Battalion, 6th Armored Division, observes the fall of shot from beside his vehicle, nicknamed *Care Free II*, during the fighting near Koltzchen on 15 April.

This Jagdpanzer 38(t) Hetzer was knocked out during the fighting against the 99th Division in the Ruhr pocket in mid-April. It has suffered an internal ammunition explosion, which has blown off its roof.

Another view of one of the relatively rare M36B1 90mm gun motor carriages, in this case serving with the 654th Tank Destroyer Battalion in support of the 35th Division, Ninth Army. The four small Nazi flags on the mantlet are victory markings for the two Pz.Kpfw. IV's and two Tigers knocked out by this vehicle. This M36B1 has duckbill end connectors fitted to its track for better flotation in muddy conditions.

An M18 76mm gun motor carriage enters Düsseldorf, Germany, in April. This shows the less common configuration with the muzzle brake. The crew has rigged a shelf across the front of the vehicle for additional stowage.

The company of Jagdtiger tank destroyers of schwere Panzer Jäger Abteilung 512 (512th Heavy Tank Destroyer Battalion) led by Hauptmann (Captain) Ernst fought for several days against the 3rd Armored Division and other American units around Paderborn in mid-April. The company finally surrendered on 16 April in Iserlohn after the envelopment of the Ruhr pocket. Three of the remaining Jagdtigers were formed up in the town square for the surrender to troops of the 99th Infantry Division. The nearest Jagdtiger has two kill bands on its barrel.

The vehicles of Ernst's Jagdtiger company are seen here from the opposite direction of the previous photo, with a pair of Sd.Kfz. 251 Ausf. D in the foreground. These are apparently Sd.Kfz. 251/18 Beobachtungspanzerwagen, used as observation vehicles for the company with the FuG 12 radio set.

Ernst's Jagdtiger company lines up on 16 April in Iserlohn for the surrender ceremony.

Another view of the surrender ceremony from the scrapbook of a 99th Division veteran.

An M4A3 of Task Force Shaughnessy of Combat Command Reserve, 9th Armored Division, covers the Mulde River bridge in Colditz, Germany, on 16 April shortly after the city was captured. The operation was famous for the seizure of the Colditz fortress, which was being used as a prisoner of war camp for 1,800 Allied soldiers.

An M4A3 of the 9th Armored Division is directed over a bridge in Colditz on 16 April. The tank has a layer of spare track over the front in an untypical layout.

Engineers prepare for river-crossing operations by the 83rd Division across the Saale River on 16 April, with an M24 light tank of the 736th Tank Battalion to the right.

Engineers move an M24 Chaffee light tank over the Saale on 16 April using a pontoon ferry.

Two M24's come ashore from LCM's (landing craft, mechanized) during the Saale crossings.

An M24 on the eastern bank of the Saale following river-crossing operations of the 83rd Division on 16 April.

An M5A1 fitted with a loudspeaker is seen in operation in Magdeburg on 17 April to broadcast messages to the local civilian populace.

Resistance was not over even in the final weeks of the war. Here a squad from the 61st Armored Infantry, 10th Armored Division, dismounts from its M2A1 half-track car to continue the attack on foot near Bubenorbis, Germany, on 17 April.

Armored infantrymen of the 61st Armored Infantry Battalion ride an M4A3E8 of the 21st Tank Battalion, 10th Armored Division, during the fighting around Bubenorbis on 17 April.

An M3A1 half-track of the 61st Armored Infantry, 10th Armored Division, moves forward on 17 April. The farmhouses were set ablaze by accompanying tanks of the 21st Tank Battalion in order to suppress sniper fire.

Two T26E3 tanks of the 2nd Armored Division move through the ruins of Magdeburg on 18 April as the defense of the city was collapsing. The 2nd Armored Division began to receive the new T26E3 tanks only in the final days of March.

An M5A1 of the 3rd Armored Division engages German troops in the woods alongside the highway near Dessau on 17 April.

German troops surrender to the 99th Division during the concluding phase of the Ruhr encirclement. The vehicle in the foreground is a Volkswagen Schwimmwagen amphibious vehicle.
MILITARY HISTORY INSTITUTE

A column of German refugees passes an M4A3 (76mm) of the 771st Tank Battalion in the 84th Division's sector near Werben on 17 April.

Among the odder armored vehicles encountered in Germany were these wooden training tanks. In this case, it is a wooden replica of the Soviet T-34. This wooden T-34 training tank was built on a French Renault UE armored tractor and found near Wissenfels on 17 April.

These wooden training tanks were used for training German infantry in antitank tactics. However, during the fighting in 1945, they were often used as decoys.

This front view of the T-34 training tank shows that it is mounted on a captured French Renault UE armored tractor.

Another example of a T-34 training tank found near Molsheim. As can be seen, they varied considerably in detail and design.

Yet another variation of the T-34 training tank, in this case being inspected by military police of the 26th Division near Fulda on 3 April.

Not all the training tanks were modeled on the T-34. This one vaguely resembles the British Valentine.

An M4A3E8 passes the wreckage of a burning German truck during the April fighting in Germany.

An M10 3-inch gun motor carriage of the 823rd Tank Destroyer Battalion, Ninth Army, passes through the ruins of Magdeburg on 18 April. This vehicle has roof armor fitted as well as an extensive array of sandbag or concrete armor on the bow.

An M4A3 (76mm) HVSS of the 21st Tank Battalion, 10th Armored Division, passes by a burning German farm house on the outskirts of Rosewalden, Germany, on 20 April. The house had been set on fire after the tanks had shot at German snipers in the attic.

A new M4A3E8 (76mm) tank of the 12th Armored Division crosses a railroad track near Unterlaimbach on the main highway to Neustadt am der Aisch on 20 April. It has a length of corduroy matting on the hull side.

Some M4A3 tanks were converted for special roles. This vehicle was modified by the addition of a loudspeaker system, including a power generator in a container at the turret rear. It was used by Task Force Griffiths of the 7th Armored Division in hopes of getting German troops to surrender rather than fight.

A column of new M4A3E8 tanks of Company B, 43rd Tank Battalion, Combat Command A, 12th Armored Division, on the approaches to Nuremberg on 16 April.

A heavily sandbagged M4 of the 2nd Armored Division advances through Magdeburg during the fighting on 18 April.

Infantry advance in support of an M4A3E8 tank during the operations in Rosswalden by the 21st Tank Battalion, 10th Armored Division, on 20 April.

An M4A3 (76mm) of the 191st Tank Battalion provides fire support for the 180th Infantry, 45th Division, during street-clearing operations in Nuremberg on 19 April.

A pair of M4A3 tanks of the 21st Tank Battalion, 10th Armored Division, take part in the advance near Rosswalden on 20 April.

A sandbagged M4A3 (76mm) of the 756th Tank Battalion supporting the 15th Infantry, 3rd Infantry Division, during the fighting in Nuremberg on 19 April.

Three M4A3E8 (76mm)'s and a lone M4 move through the rubble in the northern portion of Nuremberg on 20 April, the day the garrison finally surrendered. Several days earlier, the 14th Armored Division defeated the small armored contingent defending the city, Gruppe Grafenwehr, an improvised force of thirty-five tanks scraped together from local factories. The lead M4A3E8 has the characteristic baskets for sand bags of the 14th Armored Division while the two behind it are probably replacements received after the February–March sandbag project. The old M4 tank to the right has an unusual pattern of appliqué armor on the hull side.

Another M4A3E8 (76mm) of the 14th Armored Division in Nuremberg on 20 April, with the sandbag basket on the turret side, but lacking the usual frame on the hull side or the front sand bags.

An M4A3 (76mm) of the 191st Tank Battalion prowls through the rubble of Nuremberg on a sniper hunt on 20 April while supporting operations of the 45th Division.

A view farther down the street as the M4A3 (76mm) continues its sniper hunt in Nuremberg with the aid of riflemen of the 45th Division.

A beat-up old M4A1 of the 191st Tank Battalion crunches its way through the rubble of Nuremberg on 20 April. This battalion had seen combat in North Africa and the Italian theater and had a number of old veteran tanks like this one, still in service after more than two years of combat.

The 45th Division held an impromptu parade in Nuremberg on 21 April to celebrate the capture of the city. Here two M4A3 (76mm) tanks of the 191st Tank Battalion pass by. These have the usual Seventh Army racks for sand bags.

An M4 105mm assault gun of HQ Company, 66th Armored Infantry Battalion, Combat Command A, 7th Armored Division, passes through a fortified gate in the old town of Dinkelsbuhl on 21 April.

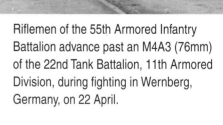

Riflemen of the 55th Armored Infantry Battalion advance past an M4A3 (76mm) of the 22nd Tank Battalion, 11th Armored Division, during fighting in Wernberg, Germany, on 22 April.

A GI looks over a 2cm flak cannon mounted in a concrete parapet for train defense on a train captured in Germany in April. These types of protected mounts were used on armored trains as well as on regular transport trains for self-defense against Allied fighter-bombers.

In the final weeks of the war, American troops frequently encountered flak trains that were used to protect railyards and trains that might be attacked by Allied fighter-bombers. One of the standard configurations for the tactical flak trains used two of these distinctive round reinforced-concrete turrets on either end of a flat car for their machine-gun and automatic-cannon armament. This particular train is armed with triple heavy machine-gun pedestal mounts.

An especially elaborate camouflage scheme is seen on this flak train captured near Steinbach by the 12th Infantry, 14th Division, on 30 April. It was reportedly used by a senior SS officer.

A close-up showing the typical concrete tower of these flak trains.

A flak train armed with 88mm guns captured on 2 May in Germany.

Among the more unusual vehicles captured in the Beyreuth area on 23 April was this Panzerattrapen, a prewar training tank consisting of an automobile with a false body attached to it.

A special version of the Hummel 150mm self-propelled gun called the Geschützwagen III/IV für Munition was fielded on a scale of two per battery of six Hummels. The Munitionsträger was essentially similar to the Hummel, except for the lack of the gun and the plated-over opening on the superstructure. This example of a Munitionsträger was captured by the U.S. Fifteenth Army in the Ruhr in 1945.

A rear view of one of the rare Munitionsträger captured in the Ruhr.

Riflemen of the 71st Infantry, 44th Division, ride on the back of an M4A3E8 of the 772nd Tank Battalion across the Danube near Berg on 23 April.

An M4A3 tank of the 25th Tank Battalion, 14th Armored Division, in Germany in April. This is probably a replacement tank as it lacks the usual Seventh Army sandbag racks.

An M4A3E8 of the 6th Armored Division crosses a bridge over the Mulde River in Rochlicht in April.

A solider of the 69th Division poses on a captured 150mm Hummel self-propelled gun near Wurzen on 25 April during the operations along the Mulde. The Hummel was the standard German heavy self-propelled gun in 1944–45.

GIs from the 10th Armored Division look over a late-production Panther Ausf. G in April.

One of the new M4A3 (105mm) assault guns with the new horizontal volute spring suspension (HVSS) in the Ninth Army's sector in April.

A column of M4A3E8 tanks of the 25th Tank Battalion, 14th Armored Division, clanks through the streets of Eichstadt in southern Germany on 25 April.

Obsolete tanks occasionally appeared on the battlefield, especially in the desperate days of the spring of 1945. This Pz.Kpfw. 35(t) was knocked out by the 704th Tank Destroyer Battalion in Germany in 1945.

A pair of Pz.Kpfw. IV knocked out on their rail transport in the Nennig railyard in 1945. The second tank has had its superstructure blown away.

Infantry from the 14th Armored Division move through Gungolding, Germany, after crossing the Altmuhl River on 26 April. The M2A1 half-track car is from the 807th Tank Destroyer Battalion and is being followed by an M20 armored utility car and an M8 armored car.

An M4A3 approaches a burning German truck during the fighting near Lackenhauser on the Austrian border on 26 April.

Tanks of the newly arrived 20th Armored Division wait to cross the Danube near Zirgesheim on 26 April. Besides the M4A3 tanks in the center of the photo, some of the new M24 light tanks can be seen to the left.

An infantry column is halted by a stalled M4A3 (76mm) from Company B, 43rd Tank Battalion, 12th Armored Division, which has slid off the road near Schwabmünchen on 27 April.

The highway provides smooth sailing for an M18 Hellcat carrying GIs of the 63rd Division near Scheppech, Germany, on 27 April. The M18 was the fastest U.S. Army tracked armored fighting vehicles of the war, capable of road speeds of 45 miles per hour. This vehicle is fitted with the M1A1C or M1A2 76mm gun with a muzzle brake.

The M20 command car of Maj. Gen. Clarence Huebner, commander of the V Corps, near Torgau, Germany, on 27 April when the U.S. Army and the Red Army met along the Elbe River. This vehicle has many small modifications, including a step on the bow and ladders on the side to make it easier for the officers to get in and out. It also has a plastic windscreen added.

An M24 light tank of the 756th Tank Battalion sits at a crossroads in Augsberg while supporting the 3rd Infantry Division. The city surrendered the day before, 27 April.

An M5A1 of Troop D 116th Cavalry Recon Squadron, 12th Armored Division, pushes through Heim on 28 April.

The Bavarian capital of Munich was a special prize for the U.S. Army, having been the wellspring of the Nazi movement. The city was surrounded by Patton's Third Army and Patch's Seventh Army, with elements of both the 20th Armored and 12th Armored Divisions pushing into the outskirts of the city. This shows a column of tanks of the 12th Armored Division led by an M4A1 (76mm) in Munich on 29 April before the collapse of German resistance the following day.

The crew of an M36 90mm tank destroyer throw food to some liberated Allied prisoners of war in the outskirts of Munich on 29 April shortly before German resistance in the city finally collapsed.

This Jagdtiger of schwere Panzer Jäger Abteilung 653 (653rd Heavy Tank Destroyer Battalion) was knocked out by a concerted attack of five M4 tanks of the 14th Armored Division near Munich. An ammunition fire ripped the roof off.

An M7 105mm howitzer motor carriage from Battery C, 414th Armored Field Artillery Battalion, 20th Armored Division, passes in front of the town clock tower in Aichach near Munich on 29 April, with white surrender flags seen in several windows. This is a late-production M7 105mm howitzer motor carriage with the E8546 transmission cover.

An increasingly common event in the final weeks of fighting was the decision by German townspeople to declare their town "open" and put out white flags. This late in the war, American armored infantry was in no mood to engage in street fighting, and if resistance was encountered, the town was liable to be pummeled by artillery. Here an armored infantry battalion from the 20th Armored Division moves through Aichach, Germany, on the outskirts of Munich on 29 April.

An M16 of the 354th Anti-Aircraft Artillery Automatic Weapons Battalion carries out its usual mission of covering a bridge over the Lech River while supporting the 103rd Division near Schöngau, Germany, on 29 April.

The encirclement of Army Group B in the Ruhr enabled the U.S. Army to race into central and southern Germany. Many infantry units used their attached tank and tank destroyer battalions to form mobile task forces to speed the advance, like this squad from the 328th Infantry, 26th Division, riding an M4A3 (76mm) tank of the 778th Tank Battalion on 29 April while moving on the Ilz River.

A StuG III Ausf. G with *Saukopf* mantlet found near Weimar at the end of the war. The gun appears to be in full recoil.

An M24 light tank of Company D, 27th Tank Battalion, 20th Armored Division, moves down the streets of Munich on 30 April. The 20th Armored Division was one of the last American armored divisions to enter combat—on 24 April.

The main objective of the U.S. Seventh Army was the Bavarian capital of Munich. Here a column of Shermans led by an M4A1 (76mm) form up in the outskirts of the city for a march into the city square on 30 April. Munich had been heavily damaged by previous bomber raids.

With the end of resistance in Munich on 30 April, an M4 tank of the 9th Tank Battalion, 20th Armored Division, moves through the streets of the city to the waves of Germans civilians relieved that the war is finally over.

A column of M4 tanks from the 10th Armored Division moves through the picturesque town of Garmisch-Partkirchen in the foothills of the Alps south of Munich on 30 April as part of the 6th Army Group's drive through Bavaria. The second and fourth tanks are the newer M4A3E8 (76mm).

Troops of the 113th Cavalry Group greet Soviet troops after meeting at Appollensdorf on 30 April.

Troops of the 105th Engineer Combat Battalion look over some old Pz.Kpfw. III's in the repair yard near the Krupp Grusonwerk tank factory after its capture.

A rare view of a column of M7B1 105mm howitzer motor carriages moving toward a burning German town in April. The M7B1's can be distinguished by the longer hull sides and by the rear plate. They are fitted with duckbill extended end connectors and are towing M8 armored ammunition trailers. Few appear to have been deployed in Europe.

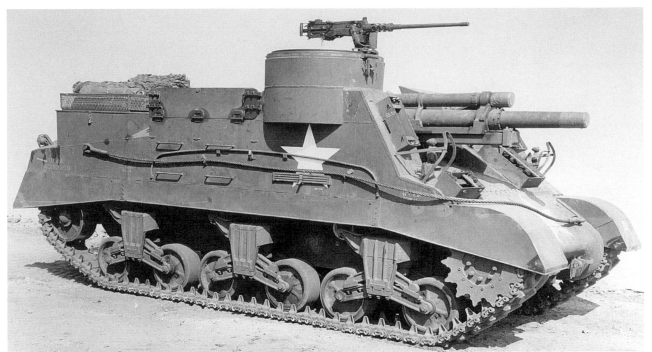

A detail view of the M7B1 during trials in the United States. This version resembled the late-production M7 105mm howitzer motor carriage.

This overhead view of an M7B1 on trials at Fort Knox illustrates the difference of the M7B1 from the late M7, notably the distinctive air intake grills present on the M7B1 but absent on the M7.

The main difference between the M7B1 and the older M7 was the engine. The M7 was based on the M4 tanks with Continental radial engine while the M7B1 was based on the M4A3 tank chassis with the Ford GAA engine. This is evident from the rear from the difference in exhausts.

The M4A3 (105mm) with horiztonal volute spring suspension (HVSS) was the latest version of this assault gun to enter service in the spring of 1945 and was not widely photographed. This one is towing the usual ammunition trailer during operations in Germany in April.

Although American and British tanks seldom operated alongside each other in the European theater, American combat photographers occasionally got a shot of British tanks when operating along the combat perimeter of the U.S. Ninth Army, which fought alongside Montgomery's British/Canadian 21st Army Group. This is a Churchill infantry tank during the Rhine operations in April.

The 6th Armored Division began receiving the M24 in late April. This was a comparison done to show the difference with the older M5A1 light tank.

A forward view of one of the new M24 light tanks of the 6th Armored Division.

An M24 light tank in 6th Armored Division service in late April.

CHAPTER 6

On to Berlin

ALTHOUGH ALLIED PLANNING had long assumed that Berlin was "the main prize," Gen. Dwight Eisenhower backed away from this objective in March 1945 when Berlin was assigned to the Soviet occupation zone at the Yalta conference. Gen. Omar Bradley estimated that a Berlin attack would cost 100,000 casualties, and Eisenhower judged this "a pretty stiff price for a prestige objective." The Red Army was 30 to 40 miles from Berlin while British and American units were more than 200 miles away. The ultimate dividing line with the Red Army in April was the Elbe River. The first of the western Allied forces to approach Berlin was Gen. William Simpson's U.S. Ninth Army, which reached the river on 12 April near Tangermünde, 53 miles from Berlin. On 15 April, Simpson conferred with Bradley about making a thrust for Berlin, but Eisenhower instructed them to consolidate their positions and wait for the Red Army. The first contact with the Red Army on the Elbe was made near Torgau on 25 April.

Curiously enough, Eisenhower's final plans contained the frequent mention of the National Redoubt (or Alpine Redoubt) as a secondary operational objective. This myth had emerged in Allied planning in December 1944 and was based on the presumption that the Nazis would make their last stand in the Bavarian Alps south of Munich, where the Nazi movement was first born. Eisenhower's headquarters became convinced that a significant threat existed of prolonged German resistance in the Bavarian Alps even after Germany's main forces had been defeated. As a result, Gen. Jacob Devers's 6th Army Group and elements of Gen. George Patton's Third Army were directed southeastward at the end of April 1945 to clear out any potential resistance centers. In fact, there was no scheme for a National Redoubt, but the effort pushed Allied forces into northwest Austria near Obersalzburg and Linz and across the Czechoslovakian border. Patton's advance southeastward out of Bayreuth raised the issue of whether Allied forces should attempt to liberate Prague. Eisenhower instructed Patton not to race to Prague and to leave it to the Red Army. With nearly all of Germany overrun and Hitler dead, the remnants of the German government sued for peace.

The final campaign in the first week of May 1945 saw little heavy combat, though pockets of resistance remained. Many of the photos here are of the many and varied types of German weapons discovered when Allied forces captured the last German strongholds.

A jeep from the medical detachment of the 704th Tank Destroyer Battalion passes by an abandoned Jagdpanzer 38(t) in western Czechoslovakia after Patton's Third Army moved across the border in the final week of the war. PATTON MUSEUM

A combat engineer battalion begins work on a pontoon bridge over the Isar River in Bavaria to replace the Moosburg bridge demolished by the retreating Wehrmacht. In the foreground are a pair of M4A3 (76mm) tanks, the one on the right with some of its sandbag armor knocked off.

An M4A3E8 of the 14th Armored Division in southern Germany on 1 May. This is probably a replacement tank that was received after February–March 1945, when the division fitted most of its tanks with the Seventh Army–style sandbag cages.

A column of M4A3 tanks of the 191st Tank Battalion take a break along the highway in May.

American troops of the 80th Division meet a tank unit of the Red Army on the Elbe in April, with a T-34-85 tank across the bridge.

A Soviet T-34-85 moves across the bridge as the 80th Division meets the Red Army on the Elbe River.

The U.S. Army began bumping into the Red Army along the Elbe in late April. Occasionally, there were encounters with Soviet tank units like this emplaced T-34-85 medium tank, the Soviet equivalent of the Sherman. This one was spotted near Wismar on 3 May.

Crews of the 14th Armored Division do preventive maintenance on their new M4A3E8 tanks in May.

An M2 half-track towing a cargo trailer of the 14th Armored Division in Germany on 1 May.

Gen. Maximilian von Edelsheim of the XXXXVIII Panzer Korps crosses the Elbe in an amphibious Schwlmmwagen near Stendal to discuss surrender terms with the U.S. 102nd Division on 4 May.

An M18 76mm gun motor carriage of the 704th Tank Destroyer Battalion during operations in support of the 89th Division, First Army, in the Lossnitz Forest in May. The crew has added an addition .30-caliber Browning machine gun on the right side of the turret and stowed an extra length of track on the bow.

Swiss border guards look over an M5A1 light tank along the German frontier near Münster on 6 May.

The initial production batch of M18 gun motor carriages were returned to the factory for reworking of their transmission, and 640 were later converted into M39 armored utility vehicles, as seen here. These were intended to perform various functions, and a small number saw service in Europe in the concluding months of the war.

This overhead view of an M39 armored utility vehicle shows the layout for the crew. This vehicle was not intended as an armored infantry carrier but rather as a utility vehicle for a variety of tasks, including prime mover and cavalry reconnaissance vehicle.

A rear view of one of the M39 armored utility vehicles. These vehicles saw no significant service in World War II but were later used in small numbers in Korea.

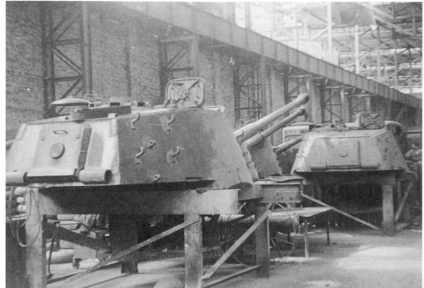

Last of the King Tigers. This is a view inside the Henschel plant in Kassel after its capture by American forces following the fighting for Paderborn.

The Germans were developing two superheavy tanks at war's end: the Maus and the E-100. The prototype for the incomplete E-100 superheavy tank was also located at the Haustenbeck proving ground and is seen here in its final state.

A view of one of the incomplete E-100 hulls found at the end of the war.

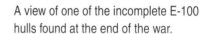

While captured M8 armored cars in German service were not particularly rare, this version certainly was. It has been reequipped with a 15mm Drilling antiaircraft cannon mount instead of its usual 37mm gun.

Another view of the M8 armored car with Drilling mount. It carried tactical number 342 on the rear side of the turret.

This M4A3 (76mm) was captured at some point by German forces and used in combat after being painted with a crude swastika for recognition purposes. It was recaptured by the 3rd Armored Division and is seen after the war in a tank work yard near Kassel.

The most powerful antitank gun at the end of the war was the German 128mm gun, though few if any saw combat service. There was a program underway since 1944 to field a dual-purpose 128mm field/antitank gun, as well as a program to quickly field surplus 128mm guns from the Jagdtiger on existing field-gun mounts. Two competitive designs were developed. This is the Krupp version of the 128mm PaK 44, also known as the PaK 80 and Kanone 44. This shows the weapon in the travel configuration.

The Rheinmetall version of the 128mm PaK 44 had a somewhat more elaborate gun shield and a six-wheel carriage configuration.

The U.S. Army found a great many unusual armored vehicle designs in the last weeks of the war, often types that had reached only prototype stage. This armored SWS half-track with 15cm Nebelwerfer rocket launchers was named *Thorn*. It is not clear if this was a one-of-a-kind prototype or part of a small production lot. The standard version of the armored SWS was intended as an ammunition carrier.

A Geschützwagen Tiger would have been the largest German armored fighting vehicles of the war, though it was never completed. It was an open-topped self-propelled artillery vehicle that was planned to accommodate a variety of heavy artillery weapons. The first assembled, the Gerat 809, was intended for the 170mm K72. A single pilot was in the final stages of construction in the spring of 1945 when it was captured by the U.S. Army.

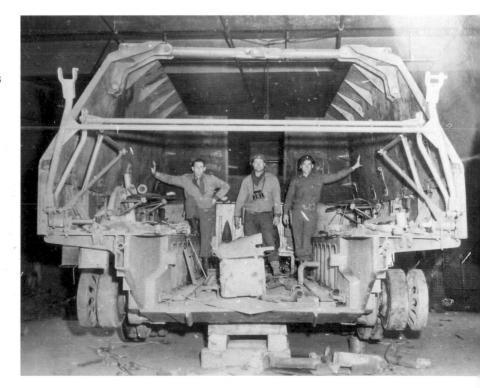

The basic version of the armored SWS half-track was intended to be used to carry quad 20mm or single 37mm flak automatic cannon. Although some of the unarmored SWS Flakwagen were deployed before the war's end, few, if any, of the armored versions were completed.

An overhead photo from an American technical intelligence report showing the rear bed of the armored SWS where the flak-gun mounting would be attached.

American troops inspect a number of German armored fighting vehicle production facilities in the weeks after the war's end. Here a trainload of uncompleted Hetzer hulls wait outside the main Skoda assembly hall in Plzen (Pilsen), Czechoslovakia.

This Jagdpanzer 38 was also found at the Skoda plant in May but is from the initial summer 1944 production batches with the typical Skoda-pattern ambush camouflage.

This pair of Jagdpanzer 38's was found at the Rheinmetall proving ground at Hillersleben; the vehicle to the right is one of the rare Jagdpanzer 38 Starr's with its narrow mantlet. This photo is doubly rare, as few Starr vehicles ever left Czech territory. The Starr version was an attempt to develop a simpler and less expensive recoil system for the Hetzer.

A variety of rare panzers was captured in the final weeks of the war as Germany collapsed. This tracked reconnaissance vehicle was the Aufklärer Pz.Kpfw. 38(t), which placed the 20mm Hangelafette 38 turret on the Czechoslovak 38(t) chassis.

One of the more obscure German tank destroyers to enter service in 1945 was this lightweight design. Steyr proposed an inexpensive tank destroyer mating the PaK 40 75mm gun to the Raupenshlepper Ost (RSO) tracked prime mover with a simple armored cab.

Another view of the tank destroyer version of the RSO tractor. As can be seen, the driver's position had armor plates that folded down for protection when the gun was fired over the front. Otherwise, the blast would damage the glass instrument faces on the dashboard.

An overhead view of an RSO tank destroyer showing the PaK 40 75mm antitank gun mounting and the rear travel lock.

A more commonly encountered tank destroyer in the winter of 1944–45 was the Sd.Kfz. 251/22, which mounted the 75mm PaK 40 on the standard army half-track. This particular vehicle belonged to the 11th Panzer Division, which fought for much of the campaign against the Seventh and Third Armies.

Another view of the Sd.Kfz. 251/22. The 11th Panzer Division's insignia can be seen on the hull rear.

An overhead view of the Sd.Kfz. 251/22 showing the PaK 40 mounting. Notice the spare ammunition to the left of the gun in the usual transport tubes.

This armored train was captured by U.S. forces near Hagenow, Germany, in May. The nearest flat car carries a turreted 10.5cm leFH18 and behind it is a car with a 2cm FlaK 38 mounting. These trains were not commonly used on the Western Front, and this may be a train that had retreated from the Eastern Front, where they were widely used in antipartisan warfare.

This shows the other end of the armored train armed with a flat car mounting a Pz.Kpfw. IV turret.

An armored column from Patton's Third Army advances into Austria near Lembach on 3 May. The M4A3 (76mm) is fitted with appliqué armor on the turret and on the hull front.

An M8 armored car of the 125th Cavalry Recon Squadron is the focus of attention following the liberation of the Luckenwalde POW camp on 3 May.

The 704th Tank Destroyer Battalion of the 4th Armored Division captured this German train that was hauling armored equipment from the front in western Czechoslovakia. The most curious item is the StuG III Ausf. G at the left. This vehicle had been provided to the Romanian army before it switched sides in the summer of 1944. In September 1944, Romanian armored vehicles, now allied with the Red Army, were repainted with white circles and red stars as seen here. The Romanians fought on the Soviet side for the remainder of the war and apparently lost this StuG III to a German unit sometime in the spring of 1945.

The 11th Panzer Division surrendered to the U.S. Army on 4 May in Bavaria. Among the vehicles turned over were these late-production Panther Ausf. G's. They feature the small oval hooks on the turret sides for attaching camouflage that were added on the production lines starting in March 1945.

An M36 90mm gun motor carriage of the 601st Tank Destroyer Battalion moves through Berchtesgaden near Hitler's mountain retreat carrying troops of the 3rd Infantry Division on 4 May. The 601st was the longest-serving tank destroyer unit of the war, having fought at El Guettar in the North African campaign in 1943. It was attached to the 3rd Infantry Division for most of the European campaign. Its insignia, a black Y on a yellow square, is evident in this view.

Another find on the German train in Czechoslovakia was this late-production StuG III Ausf. G complete with *Saukopf* mantlet and the added concrete armor on the front, with two medics from the 704th Tank Destroyer Battalion posing in front of it.

An M3 half-track from a 13th Armored Division column enters Gschaid in Bavaria on 2 May.

An M4 of the 7th Armored Division dips its tracks into the Baltic near Rehna on 3 May.

American units began bumping into Red Army units along the Elbe in April. This Soviet Lend-Lease M4A2 (76mm) was encountered by the 82nd Airborne Division near Grabow, Germany, on 3 May. The slogan painted on the hull side is *Vpered k pobede!*—"Forward to victory!"

Armored infantrymen of the 11th Armored Division advance under the watchful eye of a T26E3 tank during the operations near Neufelden, Austria, on 4 May. The 11th operated more T26E3 tanks than any other unit, receiving thirty-two of these new tanks in May.

The Allied fronts in Europe met up on 4 May with the surrender of German forces along the Brenner Pass between Austria and northern Italy. A pair of M5A1 of the 757th Tank Battalion of the Fifth Army sets up a roadblock in one of the towns in the pass.

The relaxed attitude of these young German soldiers is the clearest indication that the war is over. In the foreground is an M10 3-inch gun motor carriage of the 824th Tank Destroyer Battalion, and behind are some M5A1 light tanks of Company D, 757th Tank Battalion.

Italian POWs return to Italy through the Brenner Pass in early May, guarded by a heavily sandbagged M4A3E8's of the 781st Tank Battalion, Seventh Army.

Another view of the Seventh Army checkpoint in the Brenner Pass on 4 May.

Troops of the 11th Armored Division fire on German positions in the town of Keppel, Austria, on 4 May. The M4A3 (76mm) in this picture is fitted with appliqué armor on the turret front and probably the hull front as well.

An M4A3E8 of the 11th Armored Division fords the Muhl River at the head of a column advancing into Neufelden, Austria, on 4 May.

An M4A3 HVSS 105mm howitzer motor carriage of the 13th Armored Division crosses a pontoon bridge between Germany and Austria. The new version of the 105mm howitzer tank with horizontal volute spring suspension was not common until the final months of the war in Europe.

The last armored division to arrive in the European theater was the 20th Armored Division. Here a couple of its M4A1 tanks ford a river on the outskirts of Salzburg in Austria on 4 May.

A rifleman of the 103rd Division advances alongside a M4A3E8 of the 781st Tank Battalion on the approaches to Innsbruck, Austria.

An M24 light tank of the 20th Armored Division on the way to Salzburg, with a pair of burning Bergepanther tank-recovery vehicles in the background on 4 May.

An M5A1 of the 705th Tank Destroyer Battalion in Lembach, Germany, on 4 May posing for photographers as it runs over a Nazi banner. Some tank destroyer battalions used M5A1's in lieu of the unpopular M8 light armored car, but this was not standard at this stage of the war.

A column of M4A3 tanks of the 778th Tank Battalion negotiates a corduroy log road along the Czechoslovakian border on 6 May.

American troops visit the bombed remains of the MNH tank plant in Hannover, where the Panther tank was assembled.

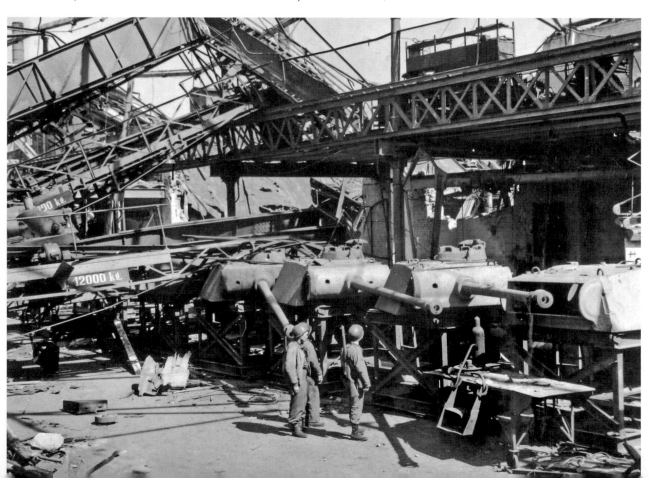

Czech officials meet with troops of the 4th Armored Division near Pisek on 9 May near an M4A3E2 (76mm) assault tank.

A close-up of the M4A3E2 seen above shows it to be the upgraded version with the 76mm gun substituted for the usual 75mm gun and a .50-caliber aircraft machine gun in place of the usual .30-caliber coaxial machine gun.

A scout jeep and M24 in Pisek, Czechoslovakia, in May.

A jubilant crowd of political prisoners and slave laborers greet an M8 light armored car of the 11th Armored Division following the liberation of the Mauthausen concentration camp on 6 May.

There was some territorial swapping as the U.S. Army adjusted its occupation zone with the Red Army. This pair of T-34 Model 1943 tanks are part of the Red Army contingent taking over Leipzig from the Seventh Army on 7 July 1945.

Patton's Third Army was authorized to enter Czechoslovakia in May but told to stay out of Prague. Here a pair of M24 light tanks of the 9th Armored Division takes up positions for an eventual parade in Karlsbad on 10 May.

A Soviet Lend-Lease M4A2 (76mm) Sherman encountered at the border of the occupation zone in Austria in the weeks after the war's end.

The tanks of the 736th Tank Battalion hold a review in the town square of Piene on 27 May. The tanks have been cleaned up and given a new set of markings. The tank in the lower left is one of the late-production M4A1 (76mm)'s delivered to the European theater in the spring of 1945, and the tank to the right leading the review is an M4A3E8 (76mm).

In a final review of the troops, Maj. Gen. A. C. Smith, commander of the 14th Armored Division, inspects his units along the Isar River near Moosburg on 30 May. The M4A3's have a mixture of the old vertical volute spring suspension (VVSS) and the new horizontal volute spring suspension (HVSS).

An old M4A3 of the 2nd Armored Division named *Destination?* moves through the rubble of Berlin prior to the Fourth of July victory celebration held there in 1945. The 2nd was the first American division sent into Berlin after the war to occupy the American sector there. This is an early dry-stowage vehicle and is interesting in that the turret is one of the less common styles that lack the side shell ejection port.

An M4A3 (76mm) of the 2nd Armored Division is surrounded by a crowd of curious onlookers in the Zehlendorf area of Berlin on 4 July. The tank has been cleaned up for the occasion, including the removal of the appliqué armor on the glacis plate so characteristic of this division.

An M32B3 of the 18th Tank Battalion, 8th Armored Division, is seen here on parade in Plzen, Czechoslovakia, during a Fourth of July parade in 1945.

An M24 of the 38th Cavalry Reconnaissance Squadron, 102nd Cavalry Group, takes part in a victory parade in Prague in July. Gaudy markings like the Allied stars on the bow of these tanks were painted on American vehicles for the postwar victory parades.

One of the lesser known American deployments at the end of the war was to Norway to supervise the surrender of German forces there. This is a parade by American and British forces in Oslo on 30 June.

A close-up of an M8 light armored car of the U.S. occupation troops in Oslo in June.

A number of American armored units were converted into police units for occupation duties. This M8 light armored car is seen with the 14th Constabulary Squadron at Grafenwöhr after the war.

A platoon of M26 Pershing tanks of the 10th Tank Battalion, 5th Armored Division, serve as the backdrop to Capt. Art. Whitley's wedding in Illfield on 2 June.

An advance party from the 2nd Armored Division arrives in Berlin in July to plan the arrival of the American occupation forces. They meet with their Soviet counterparts. In the background is a Lend-Lease Red Army M3A1 scout car, an American vehicle type much more widely used by the Soviet forces than the U.S. Army, which considered it obsolete.

An M7 105mm howitzer motor carriage of the 2nd Armored Division on occupation duty in Germany shortly after the end of the war in 1945. It is nicknamed, appropriately enough, *Coming Home*. This is an intermediate-production vehicle with evidence of many field mods, such as the typical 2nd Armored Division racks on the rear hull sides.

Another M7 105mm howitzer motor carriage of the 2nd Armored Division on occupation duty in Germany shortly after the end of the war. It is nicknamed *Can Do*; generally, the vehicle name corresponded with the battery letter, so this vehicle presuambly belonged to Battery C.

One of the lesser known contacts with the panzer force was near Oslo, Norway, on 10 June 1945, when British and American officers oversaw the surrender of the seventy-one remaining tanks of Panzer Brigade Norway. These are some of the unit's Pz.Kpfw. III tanks.

Some strange tanks continued to turn up after the end of the fighting. This is an old Soviet T-34 found in Nuremberg, presumably a captured example that had been shipped to Germany for training purposes.

CHAPTER 7

The Shape of Things to Come

TANK BUFFS have been fascinated for many years about the fanciful German panzers that were planned for construction in late 1945 or 1946 if the war had not ended. During the final battles in Germany, the Allies captured examples of the Maus and incomplete E-100 superheavy tanks, along with many incomplete prototypes of future designs. This chapter looks at the other side of this story, the many tanks and armored vehicles scheduled to enter U.S. Army service had the war continued.

American tanks of late 1945 vary from the mundane to the preposterous. Many projects were simply extensions of the new tanks already in service in early 1945. With the U.S. Army switching from the M5A1 to the M24 light tank and from the M4 Sherman to the M26 Pershing medium tank, plans were underway to field derivatives of these new tanks for other missions, such as self-propelled field artillery versions.

However, there were also completely new schemes, some inspired by contacts with the German Tiger heavy tank. The army ordered 1,200 T29 heavy tanks in March 1945, armed with a very impressive 105mm tank gun and protected with thick armor to rival the German King Tiger. An even more powerful T30 heavy tank with a massive 155mm tank gun was underway as well, based on an upgraded version of the T29. Far more bizarre was the T28 superheavy tank, a turretless assault gun that was so heavy that it was built on four sets of track assemblies instead of the usual two.

American armored fighting vehicles of late 1945 represented a "lost generation" of American tank design. When war ended in Europe in May 1945, then in the Pacific in August, the industrial plans for tank production abruptly changed. Contracts for the production of the new tanks came to a screeching halt. Although some development efforts dragged on into the late 1940s, funding was too thin for most of these programs to survive, and few reached production beyond a few pilot models. The start of the Cold War and the outbreak of the Korean War in 1950 changed American defense plans and led to a set of new tank programs. While some of these had connections to the 1945 plans, most were entirely new. These, not the designs of 1945, formed the basis for the American tank force of the Cold War.

This chapter provides a quick overview of the fascinating tanks and armored vehicles of the lost generation. It is by no means comprehensive, but rather a potpourri of some of the more technically interesting or outlandish projects.

The demand for heavy tanks in 1944 led ordnance to consider rebuilding the archaic M6 heavy tank with a more powerful gun. Although this never reached fruition because of the obvious obsolesence of the chassis, some idea of the potential can be seen in the form of this M6A2E1 pilot, which was used to test the turret of the new T29 heavy tank in the summer of 1945.

The desire for a heavy tank to deal with German fortifications led to a 1944 program that culminated in the T95 105mm gun motor carriage, later redesignated T28 superheavy tank. This was armed with the long T5E1 105mm gun, the most powerful American tank gun developed during the war.

As can be seen from this oblique view of Pilot No. 1, the enormous weight of the T95 required the use of four sets of tracks, essentially a pair on either side. The tracks and bogies were derived from the standard M4A3E8 components.

The T95 was a classic assault gun with a fixed superstructure and a gun mount with limited traverse. The first pilot was delivered in December 1945.

This oblique overhead view shows the extremely unconventional nature of the layout of the vehicle. It was powered by a 500-horsepower Ford GAF engine, giving it a turtle-like road speed of a mere eight miles per hour.

An overhead view of the T95 105mm gun motor carriage. The vehicle had 12-inch (305mm) forward armor, making in nearly invulnerable to frontal attack against weapons of its day.

This front view of the T95 provides a clear view of the unusual suspension with paired sets of tracks. Its combat loaded weight was ninety-five tons.

Because of its nearly fifteen-foot width, the outer sets of suspension assemblies were designed to be detachable so that the T95 could be transported by rail or ship. This shows an outer track assembly (right) and the T95 with only a single set of tracks (behind).

Another view of the T95 with its outer track assembly removed. As can be seen, the T95 could tow the outboard track assembly using cables.

One of the main concerns about the T95 was transportability. This is a 1948 trial to see if it could be shipped on a normal LST (landing ship, tank). Interest in the T28 was very limited, and the program petered out in the late 1940s.

The M26 remained the backbone of army tank units after the war in occupied Germany until the advent of the improved M46 version. This photo appears to be straight out of World War II but actually shows a Pershing during Exercise Rainbow in Germany in September 1950.

The T26E3, classified as the M26 Pershing, was intended to be the army's medium tank through the end of the 1940s. Development continued in 1945, such as this effort to develop a deep-fording kit for amphibious operations.

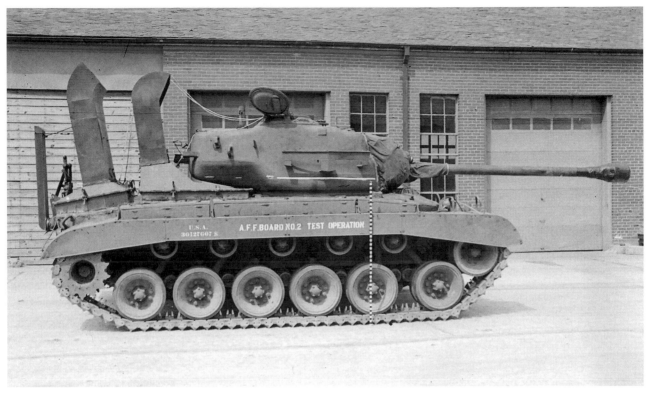

The deep-fording kit for the M26 was desired since there were plans to use the type in the invasion of Japan. A few tanks made it to Okinawa before the end of the war.

An overhead view of the M26 deep-wading kit, with the unusual small trunk attached to the rear exhaust.

In view of the poor design of wartime external machine-gun mounts on American tanks, ordnance began to examine more suitable alternatives. One of the first ideas was the T121 mount, which was fitted with two .50-caliber heavy machine guns, not only increasing firepower but also allowing the commander to operate the weapons from within protective cover.

Even though there was little enthusiasm for tank-fired artillery rockets in the armored units in the European theater, ordnance continued to tinker with the idea. This is M26 number 250, fit with the T99 4.5-inch multiple rocket launcher. As can be seen, there was a linkage between the rocket racks and the gun mount to permit the rockets to be elevated and depressed.

Mine rollers had proven to be effective, if somewhat difficult to use, during the European campaign, and work on improvements continued after the war. Since the M26 tanks were wider, an effort was made to develop a heavy mine roller for the M26 family, nicknamed the High Herman.

The 105mm assault tank had proven to be an effective complement to normal gun tanks in the European theater, so there were plans to build an assault tank armed with the same 105mm howitzer on the M26. The test version seen here was designated the T26E2, but it became the M45 105mm assault gun when accepted for production.

This overhead view of the T26E2 pilot shows the shorter gun tube as well as the use of an exhaust muffler at the rear of the hull.

This rear view shows the rear exhaust muffler on the M45. Although this tank was not ready in time for World War II, it did see service in Korea in 1950 alongside the M26 tank, with some 185 being manufactured.

The full potential of the powerful new tank guns in 1945 could not be fully realized because of their poor accuracy at longer ranges. Many armies began to consider the need for optical rangefinders to provide better ballistic correction data for long-range engagements. This is one of the T25 pilots reconfigured with a massive T31 rangefinder for trials after the war.

A tank-recovery version of the Pershing began in 1944 as the T12, which had a very substantial boom crane.

The T12 tank-recovery vehicle had entrenching spades at front and rear to stabilize the platform when doing heavy lifting and winching operations. In the event, the type never entered production.

The U.S. Army failed to field a dedicated armored engineer vehicle during World War II, but development began after the war as the T39 engineer armored vehicle. It was armed with a British 6.5-inch (165mm) demolition gun and had a special rear crane for dealing with obstacles and other tasks. It never entered production.

The proliferation of German heavy panzers during the war led to interest in an American counterpart, and the T29 heavy tank project ensued. It was armed from the outset with the T5E1 105mm gun, as seen here on the first pilot. The gun mantlet was 8 to 11 inches (205 to 280 millimeters) thick and the forward turret armor was 7 inches (180 millimeters).

Although the T29 used some components from the M26 Pershing family, it was substantially larger, as can be seen in this side view of the first pilot with its turret to the rear and gun locked in travel mode. Its heavy weight and poor fuel efficiency led to the use of drop tanks on the rear fenders.

On 1 March 1945, the army recommended the production of 1,200 T29 heavy tanks. With the end of the war in Europe in May 1945, these plans were dropped. This shows the tank with the turret in the usual battle position.

The T29 was powered by a 700-horsepower Ford GAC engine with a road range of about 100 miles. A pair of auxiliary fuel tanks was developed that could be dropped prior to combat.

Left: An overhead shot of the first T29 pilot showing the layout. Right: Another overhead photo of the T29 pilot showing the turret in the travel position with the gun barrel resting in the travel lock.

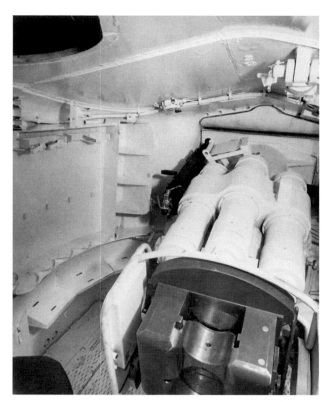 

Left: A view inside the left side of the T29, where one of the two loaders was stationed. Right: A view on the right side of the T29 turret, where the gunner and second loader were stationed.

The turret interior of the T29 heavy tank was so massive that the commander sat quite some distance to the rear, with two large stowage bins in front of him, including the 105mm ready racks.

In parallel to the T29, the T30 heavy tank was developed but armed with the 155mm T7 gun, the largest-caliber tank gun ever deployed on an American tank. In the event, development work on the T29 and T30 petered out in the late 1940s because of lack of funding.

By the time the T30 entered testing, the inadequacy of the Ford GAF on the T29 was apparent, so the T30 was powered by the 810-horsepower AV-1790-3 engine. In this view, the turret is in the travel position to the rear.

The powerful guns on the T29 and T30 needed a more sophisticated rangefinder to enjoy their full potential at long range. This is the T29E3 pilot that was fitted with a T31E1 stereoscopic rangefinder in front of the commander with the large sighting ports protruding from the turret sides.

Interest in the greater gun accuracy offered by stereoscopic rangefinders led to extensive experiments, even on the Sherman tank, as seen here at Aberdeen Proving Ground after the war.

Although there were plans to end Sherman production in favor of the Pershing, there was still some interest to develop Sherman variants suitable for the expected invasion of Japan. The T33 flamethrower tank consisted of the thickly armored M4A3E2 assault tank with new horizontal volute spring suspension (HVSS) and a new turret that permitted the use of a 75mm gun and a coaxial E20 flame gun. There were plans to build 600 of these, but this never materialized because the war ended.

A less complicated alternative to turret flamethrower tanks was a hull-mounted weapon. The T68 was an attempt to mate the Canadian E33 Iroquois pressurized flame gun in a turretless Sherman chassis.

An alternative to flamethrowers for bunker-busting was large-caliber rockets. The T31 demolition tank, based on the M4A3 Sherman, had a pair of T94 7.2-inch rocket launchers on either side of the turret and a 105mm howitzer in the center.

An overhead view of the T31 demolition tank. The grotesque turret on the T31 demolition tank was necessary to house the five-round revolver autoloader for the rocket launchers. These never worked very well, and the T31 soon disappeared.

A side view of the bizarre T31 demolition tank shows the huge turret.

A rear view of the T31 demolition tank.

The M24 Chaffee light tank was well received during its combat debut in 1945, and it remained the principal U.S. Army light tank through the late 1940s. The usual types of improvements were envisioned, like this scheme to fit wider tracks for better flotation in mud and soft soil conditions.

The M24 also served as the basis of experiments with overhead weapon stations. This tank is fitted with the experimental T12 twin .50-caliber mount.

With the expectation of landing the M24 during the invasion of Japan, ordnance developed the usual sort of deep-wading kit for amphibious landing operations.

Another alternative to deep-wading techniques was the development of flotation devices that could make a tank buoyant enough to swim to shore. This was a Cadillac attempt to develop a flotation system for the M24, first tested in November 1944.

The M24 Chaffee also got wrapped up in the schemes to fit artillery rocket launchers to tanks, in this case U.S. Navy 4.5-inch rockets in the T95 launcher.

The tank units wanted a dozer blade for the M24 light tank, and it finally appeared in the form of the T4 dozer blade kit.

The improved M4 dozer upgrade did make it to production, as seen on this M24 in Germany in 1946.

A light tank-recovery vehicle had been in army organization charts since 1941, but it never seemed to reach production. The T6E1 program started in 1944.

This shows the T6E1 tank-recovery vehicle in travel mode with the A-frame boom folded to the rear.

A fine study of the T6E1 tank-recovery vehicle from the front. American tank-recovery vehicles generally carried an 81mm mortar for self-defense and smoke projection.

A rear view of the T6E1 showing the A-frame in folded position.

An overhead view of the T6E1 from the rear with the A-frame in travel position.

The army was never very happy with the automotive performance of the M8 light armored car and, in 1943, started a competition for a replacement. This is the Studebaker T27 8 x 8 armored car.

A view of the Studebaker T27 from the right side. It was armed with the same 37mm gun as the older M8 since the main objective of the program was to improve cross-country performance, not firepower.

A rear view of one of the Studebaker T27 prototypes. Although the Studebaker T27 was a competent design, the army generally preferred the rival Chevrolet T28.

The competitor to the T27 was the Chevrolet T28, which used a modern 6 x 6 configuration with large tires. This was accepted for production in February 1945 as the M38 Wolfhound and would have become the next U.S. Army armored car had the war not ended.

A front view of the M38 Wolfhound during the Aberdeen Proving Ground trials in 1944.

As this photo shows, the wheels of the M38 Wolfhound were independently steered for better turning ability.

An overhead view of the M38 Wolfhound with the canvas weather cover in place.

There was some interest in developing a more heavily armed version of the M38 Wolfhound, and experiments were conducted using the turret from the M24 light tank. Although satisfactory, the decision to cancel M38 production after the war ended also led to the cancellation of this project.

The M24 was selected as the basis for a family of light armored vehicles also including light self-propelled artillery. As a result, the successor to the M7 105mm howitzer motor carriage was the M37 105mm howitzer motor carriage built on the M24 chassis. Here an M37 is seen on trails at the Yuma desert proving ground.

This overhead view of the M37 105mm howitzer motor carriage shows the spacious interior of the vehicle.

A rear view of the M37 shows the large stowage racks which were generally used to carry the obligatory camouflage nets.

The M37 was accepted for service in January 1945, but only 150 were built before the end of the war led to massive contract cancellations. They served in the Korean War and were also deployed with American forces in NATO in the early 1950s.

A significant gap in self-propelled artillery for the armored divisions was the lack of a self-propelled 155mm howitzer. This was rectified with the M41 155mm howitzer motor carriage, based on a modified M24 chassis. To permit easier access to the howitzer, it was mounted on the rear. As a result, the engine compartment was moved to the center of the vehicle.

The M41 155mm howitzer motor carriage was accepted for service in June 1945, but only eighty-five were built prior to the wave of contract cancellations.

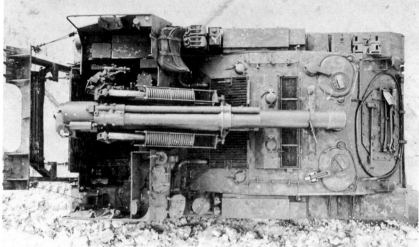

One of the pilots of the M41 on trials at the Yuma desert proving ground.

This overhead view of the M41 shows the general layout, including the mid-mounted engine and the rear recoil spade.

There was considerable interest in the potential of recoilless rifles as an alternative to conventional artillery. This was an experiment on the M41 chassis using four T21 75mm recoilless rifles. The recoilless rifle idea never proved practical because of the larger volume of propellant needed compared to conventional artillery and the awkward problems posed by the backblast of the weapons.

Although most Sherman production came to an end, the M40 155mm gun motor carriage and the related M43 8-inch howitzer motor carriage remained in production into late 1945. This is the well-known M40 "Big Shot" at Aberdeen Proving Ground, frequently shown in propaganda films of the day.

With Sherman production ending, there was interest in migrating the associated field artillery systems to the M26 tank chassis. The T84 8-inch howitzer motor carriage was the equivalent of the Sherman-based M43, but on a modified Pershing chassis.

The T84 8-inch howitzer motor carriage was a very modern self-propelled howitzer, but like so many other promising 1945 projects, it soon ended with the collapse of military funding at war's end.

The most powerful self-propelled gun developed by the U.S. Army during the war was the T92 240mm howitzer motor carriage based on heavily modified Pershing components. This photo was taken during General Robinett's visit to the Chrysler plant in June 1945.

A rear view of the T84 pilot showing the large recoil spade at the rear of the vehicle needed to help compensate for the substantial recoil of the 8-inch howitzer.

The army found that the towed superheavy weapons of the "Black Dragon" family, including the 240mm howitzer and 8-inch gun, were very awkward to move and emplace; there were hopes that a self-propelled version would make these weapons more practical. Both types were mounted on this chassis, the T92 240mm howitzer motor carriage (seen here) and the T93 8-inch gun motor carriage.

This is one of the T93 pilots, but during the firing trials seen here at Fort Bragg, the 8-inch gun tube was replaced with a 240mm howitzer tube, showing the interchangeability of the design.

A rear view of a T92 240mm howitzer motor carriage pilot showing the massive recoil spade.

An overhead view of the T92 240mm howitzer motor carriage, sometimes nicknamed the "King Kong."

Another overhead view of the T92 240mm howitzer motor carriage from a slightly more vertical angle shows that the rear compartment was quite minimal since the floor was clipped back to enable the weapon to be elevated to high angles.

A rear view of the T92 240mm howitzer motor carriage "King Kong" showing the large shell-loading frame that would be carried by four loaders.

A T92 240mm howitzer motor carriage pilot with the recoil spade down.

One of the mock-ups of the T92 240mm howitzer motor carriage showing the simplicity of the rear fighting compartment.

The T93 8-inch gun motor carriage was essentially similar to the T92 but used the long-barreled 8-inch (203mm) tube.

There was considerable interest in more modern antiaircraft vehicles, and the M24 Chaffee light tank was selected as part of the family of vehicles concept. The T77 was armed with four .50-caliber heavy machine guns.

An overhead view of the T77 showing both gunners. In action, the gunner's station were open.

During transit, the gunner's station were covered with clear Plexiglas blisters as seen here.

A more powerful alternative to quad .50-caliber machine guns was the 40mm Bofors gun, which was mounted on the M19, a design that shared a similar hull to the M41 155mm howitzer motor carriage, with the same mid-engine configuration.

An overhead view of the M19 showing the general layout.

The M19 antiaircraft vehicle was one of the handful of wartime projects to reach the production stage, with some 300 built by August 1945, when the contract was terminated. Some of these served in Korea.

There was some interest in a fully tracked infantry personnel carrier, which led to the obscure M44 armored utility vehicle, based on M24 components. It was large by later standards, carrying twenty-seven soldiers.

Only half a dozen M44 pilots were built before production ended. The vehicle in front of it, the unarmored M8 cargo tractor, finally entered production in 1950–55 for use by field artillery units to carry ammunition.

Index